O9-BTN-156

"With *Evolving in Monkey Town*, Rachel Held Evans steps onto the stage as a gifted writer, an honest storyteller, and a compelling voice in the Christian community. She represents what is most hopeful and promising in a new generation of articulate, intelligent, and faithful young leaders."

— BRIAN MCLAREN, author/speaker, www.brianmclaren.net

"These days the stories I love to read are the ones that ask questions, that live in the tension, that allow me to bring my doubt and uncertainty and join the conversation. Rachel Held Evans' *Evolving in Monkey Town* is one of those stories."

— SHAUNA NIEQUIST, author of *Cold Tangerines*
and *Bittersweet*

"This book is an argument — Rachel argues with herself, God, the Bible, and Southern fundamentalism. Somehow, though, we are the winners in this argument because we learn and watch as a young woman emerges into a maturing faith that lets the kingdom vision of Jesus reshape her life. I found myself cheering her on."

— SCOT MCKNIGHT, Karl A. Olsson Professor
in Religious Studies, North Park University

"Rachel Held Evans is brilliant, gutsy, real, and hilarious, and *Evolving in Monkey Town* impacted my spiritual journey in ways I never imagined. I can't remember a book that I enjoyed reading more, partly because Rachel is a great writer, and partly because she so fearlessly examines the conflict between her inherited beliefs about God and the truth of her own spiritual experience.

There's a certain weight to *Evolving in Monkey Town* that distinguishes it from the other spiritual memoir books out there."

—JIM PALMER, author of *Divine Nobodies*
and *Wide Open Spaces*

"Can I tell you how much I admire Rachel Held Evans? She is smart, compassionate, funny, and relentlessly inquisitive. It is the questions she asks, not the answers she uncovers, that make *Evolving in Monkey Town* such a compelling read. There are many good books worth reading, but a truly remarkable book will leave you pondering matters long after the cover is closed. I loved this book. That Evans wrote a remarkable debut at such a young age makes me want to slap her, bless her heart."

—KAREN SPEARS ZACHARIAS, author of *Will Jesus Buy Me a
Double-Wide?: ('Cause I Need More Room for My Plasma TV)*

"It's not every day that a book with the word 'monkey' in the title challenges and encourages me like Rachel Held Evans' debut. She adds a fresh, courageous voice to the faith-and-doubt discussion, and it's a voice all of us need to hear."

—JASON BOYETT, author of *O Me of Little Faith:
True Confessions of a Spiritual Weakling*

"*Evolving in Monkey Town* is the kind of book I'll pass along. Rachel Held Evans so accurately highlights her struggles to have a genuine, life-changing, world-beautifying faith. I love her heart, her journey, her questions, and her tentative understanding of Jesus. I'll be thinking about this book and its message for months and years to come. An important read."

—MARY DEMUTH, author of *Thin Places: A Memoir*

"When we find ourselves asking tough questions, sometimes we want answers, but many times we just want a friend who is asking the same questions we are. Written with refreshing honesty, Rachel Held Evans' new book *Evolving in Monkey Town* is going to be that friend for many people."

— CHAD GIBBS, author of *God and Football:*
   Faith and Fanaticism in the SEC

"Rachel's humorous yet humble memoir of growing up in the evangelical world serves as an encouraging guide for anyone looking to navigate through that particular subculture. As I saw my own journey reflected in its pages, I appreciated Rachel's honesty in revealing the doubts and questions that arose when she confronted the cracks in the evangelical facade. The story told here is both faith and doubt affirming, a beautiful reflection of a heart earnestly seeking to follow God fully."

— JULIE CLAWSON, author of *Everyday Justice:*
   The Global Impact of Our Daily Choices

"A whole generation of evangelicalism's brightest young people, based upon a common misunderstanding of 1 Peter 3:15, was taught that vital, living faith is established by a 'worldview' that one can explain and defend. Rachel Held Evans, a bright and talented young writer with obvious courage, challenges this 'sacred cow.' Her discovery is surely right — we need a faith that obeys, not a worldview rooted in absolute certainty. She will help you embrace the questions without losing the reality of faith."

— JOHN H. ARMSTRONG, president of ACT 3
   and author of *Your Church Is Too Small*

FAITH
UNRAVELED

FAITH
UNRAVELED

HOW *a* GIRL WHO KNEW ALL *the* ANSWERS
LEARNED *to* ASK QUESTIONS

Previously titled *Evolving in Monkey Town*

Rachel Held Evans

Bestselling author of *A Year of Biblical Womanhood*

ZONDERVAN

Faith Unraveled
Copyright © 2010 by Rachel Held Evans

Previously published as *Evolving in Monkey Town*

This title is also available as a Zondervan ebook. Visit www.zondervan.com/ebooks.

Requests for information should be addressed to:

Zondervan, 3900 *Sparks Drive SE, Grand Rapids, Michigan* 49546

This edition: ISBN 978-0-310-33916-8 (softcover)

Library of Congress Cataloging-in-Publication Data

Evans, Rachel Held, 1981–
      Evolving in Monkey Town : how a girl who knew all the answers learned to ask the
questions / Rachel Held Evans.
        p. cm.
      ISBN 978-0-310-29399-6 (softcover)
      1. Evans, Rachel Held, 1981– 2. Christian biography—United States. I. Title.
BR1725.E92A3 2010
277.3'083092—dc22 [B]   2010002107

All Scripture quotations, unless otherwise indicated, are taken from The Holy Bible, *New Interna-tional Version®, NIV®.* Copyright © 1973, 1978, 1984 by Biblica, Inc.® Used by permission of Zonder-van. All rights reserved worldwide. Scripture quotations marked NASB are taken from the *New American Standard Bible.* Copyright © 1960, 1962, 1963, 1968, 1971, 1972, 1973, 1975, 1977, 1995 by The Lockman Foundation. Used by permission. Scripture quotations marked NKJV are taken from the New King James Version. Copyright © 1982, by Thomas Nelson, Inc. Used by permission. All rights reserved. Scripture quotations marked KJV are taken from the King James Version of the Bible.

Any Internet addresses (websites, blogs, etc.) and telephone numbers in this book are offered as a resource. They are not intended in any way to be or imply an endorsement by Zondervan, nor does Zondervan vouch for the content of these sites and numbers for the life of this book.

All rights reserved. No part of this publication may be reproduced, stored in a retrieval system, or transmitted in any form or by any means—electronic, mechanical, photocopy, recording, or any other—except for brief quotations in printed reviews, without the prior permission of the publisher.

Published in association with the literary agency of WordServe Literary Group, Ltd., 10152 S. Knoll Circle, Highlands Ranch, CO 80130.

Author's note: This book is a work of nonfiction. Some names and a few identifying details have been changed to protect individuals' privacy.

Cover design: *Dual Identity*
Cover photography: *Shutterstock®*
Interior design: *Beth Shagene*

Printed in the United States of America

HB 07.30.2019

To Mom and Dad,
for believing in me enough
to make me promise at the age of eight
to dedicate my first book to you

Contents

Preface   13

Introduction: Why I Am an Evolutionist   15

PART 1 HABITAT

1. The Best Christian Attitude Award   27

2. June the Ten Commandments Lady   45

3. Monkey Town   51

4. Greg the Apologist   65

5. When Skeptics Ask   69

PART 2 CHALLENGE

6. Nathan the Soldier   83

7. When Believers Ask   89

8. Jesus, God in Sandals   101

9. Survivor's Guilt   109

10. John the Revelator   121

11. Higher Ways   127

12. Laxmi the Widow   139

13. God Things   145

14. Mark the Evangelist   157

15. Judgment Day   161

16. Adele the Oxymoron   177

17. Sword Drills   181

PART 3 CHANGE

18. Sam the Feminist   199

19. Adaptation   203

20. Dan the Fixer   213

21. Living the Questions   217

Acknowledgments   229

Notes   231

Preface

If you picked up this book looking for an objective analysis of Christianity or an unbiased interpretation of the Bible, there are a few things you probably should know first.

People tell me I exaggerate.

I tend to change my mind.

The *Stuff White People Like* blog is painfully representative of my lifestyle and habits.

I've never lived north of the Mason-Dixon Line.

Sometimes I assume that attractive women are dumb.

I've been hurt by Christians.

As a Christian, I've been hurtful.

Even though I voted for the winner of the last three elections, I've managed to feel politically marginalized each time.

I cried for an hour when I found out Tim Russert died.

I'm judgmental of people I think are judgmental.

At twenty-seven, I'm probably too young to write a memoir.

I almost always root for the underdog, and sometimes I get the feeling that God does too.

I guess what I'm trying to say is that I'm not exactly an impartial observer. My culture, my childhood, my gender, my prejudices, my hopes, my imagination, my virtues, and my vices — these things color my view of the world and infuse it with meaning. I've got baggage just like everyone else, and it's as much a part of my faith journey as the high peaks, the low valleys, and the long, lovely stretches of road that I wish could go on forever.

I'm a lot of things, but fair and balanced I am not.

So now that you know what you're getting into, read on.

Why I Am
an Evolutionist

Monkeys make me nervous. Whenever I hear about chimpanzees solving math problems or Koko the Gorilla using sign language to order her breakfast, I feel inexplicably threatened by their humanlike qualities and intelligence. I do my best to avoid the monkey exhibits at zoos and those creepy Dian Fossey documentaries on Animal Planet.

When I traveled through the Himalayan foothills of India, where wild macaques climb all over the bridges and power lines, one monkey in particular looked incredulously at my camera bag and then at me, as if to ask, Who do you think you are, lugging that fancy equipment all over a country where half the population hasn't got enough food to eat? Perhaps I read into it a bit, but I could have sworn he then turned and whispered something to his friend, who rolled his eyes at me in disgust. After that, I kept a closer eye on my camera.

I suppose my monkey-phobia has something to do with the sneaking suspicion that maybe the biologists are right after all. Maybe man and ape share a common ancestor, and that explains our eerie similarities. It's a bit disconcerting to think of modern humans arriving so late to the evolutionary scene, of God taking millions upon millions of years to get to the point. Such a scenario certainly does a number on one's pride and calls into question the notion of being created in the image of God.

To make matters worse, somewhere along the way, I was told that belief in evolutionary theory and belief in a personal, loving Creator are mutually exclusive, that if the Bible cannot be trusted to accurately explain the origins of life, it cannot be trusted for anything at all, and the Christian faith is lost. Commitment to a literal six-day creation, with the formation of Adam and Eve at its climax, held such fundamental significance to my young faith that I spent the first twenty years of my life scribbling words like *debatable* and *unlikely* in the margins of science books. I guess whenever some sly little monkey tries to undo it all with a knowing smile, I get a bit anxious.

Charles Darwin claimed that the survival or extinction of an organism is determined by its ability to adapt to its environment. Failure to adapt explains why wooly mammoths didn't survive the end of the Ice Age and why we get pigeon poop stuck on our windshields instead of dodo poop. I'm still not sure what to make of evolution. Scientists have perfectly good evidence to support it, while theologians have good biblical and philosophical reasons to be wary of its implications.

However, I have a feeling that if Darwin turns out to be right, the Christian faith won't fall apart after all. Faith is more resilient than that. Like a living organism, it has a remarkable ability to adapt to change. At our best, Christians embrace this quality, leaving enough space within orthodoxy for God to surprise us every now and then. At our worst, we kick and scream our way through each and every change, burning books and bridges and even people along the way. But if we can adjust to Galileo's universe, we can adjust to Darwin's biology — even the part about the monkeys. If there's one thing I know for sure, it's that faith can survive just about anything, so long as it's able to evolve.

I used to be a fundamentalist. Not the Teletubby-hating, apocalypse-ready, Jerry Falwell type of fundamentalist, but the kind who thinks that God is pretty much figured out already, that he's done telling us anything new. I was a fundamentalist in the sense that I thought salvation means having the right opinions about God and that fighting the good fight of faith requires defending those opinions at all costs. I was a fundamentalist because my security and self-worth and sense of purpose in life were all wrapped up in getting God right — in believing the right things about him, saying the right things about him, and convincing others to embrace the right things about him too. Good Christians, I believed, don't succumb to the shifting sands of culture. Good Christians, I used to think, don't change their minds.

My friend Adele describes fundamentalism as holding so tightly to your beliefs that your fingernails leave imprints on the palm of your hand. Adele is gay, so she knows better than most people how sharp those fingernails can be. And I think she's right. I was a fundamentalist not because of the beliefs I held but because of how I held them: with a death grip. It would take God himself to finally pry some of them out of my hands.

The problem with fundamentalism is that it can't adapt to change. When you count each one of your beliefs as absolutely essential, change is never an option. When change is never an option, you have to hope that the world stays exactly as it is so as not to mess with your view of it. I think this explains why some of the preachers on TV look so frantic and angry. For fundamentalists, Christianity sits perpetually on the precipice of doom, one scientific discovery or cultural shift or difficult theological question away from extinction. So fearful of losing their grip on faith, they squeeze the life out of it.

Fortunately, the ability to adapt to change is one of Christianity's best features, though we often overlook it. I used to think that the true Christian faith, or at least the purest version of it, started with Jesus and his disciples, took a hiatus for about a thousand years during the reign of Roman Catholicism, returned with Martin Luther and the Protestant Reformation, and fell under siege again by the modern secular humanists. I was under the impression that the most important elements of the faith had not changed over the years but had simply gotten lost and rediscovered. They were right there in the Bible, as simple and clear as could be, and it was our job as Christians to defend them and protect them from change.

But the real story of Christianity is a lot less streamlined. The real story involves centuries of upheaval, challenge, and change. From the moment Jesus floated into the clouds at his ascension, leaving his disciples standing dumbfounded on the ground,

Christians have struggled to define and apply the fundamental elements of his teachings. We haven't spent the last two thousand years simply defending the fundamentals; we've spent the last two thousand years deciding on many of them.

Things get especially heated when false fundamentals sneak into the faith and only a dramatic change in environment can root them out. Take geocentricism, for example. In Galileo's day, the church so adamantly espoused the traditional paradigm of an earth-centered universe that anyone presenting evidence to the contrary could be excommunicated. At that time, most Christians believed that the Bible speaks quite clearly about cosmology. The earth has a foundation (Job 38:4), which does not move (Ps. 93:1; Prov. 8:28). Even Protestant theologian John Calvin considered geocentricism so fundamentally true that he claimed people who believed in a moving earth were possessed by the devil.[1]

But if a geocentric universe is indeed this vital to the survival of Christianity, then Christianity would have died out with the eventual acceptance of a heliocentric cosmology. Imagine centuries of faith undone by a telescope! But instead, Christians adapted. I'm sure it took some getting used to, but believers found a way to rethink and reimagine their faith in the context of a new environment, one in which they no longer sat in the center of the universe. When the environment shifted, they chose to change their minds rather than accept extinction. In less noble terms, they decided to compromise.

While the ability to adapt to change is built into the church's DNA, letting go of false fundamentals rarely happens without a fight. The first Christians argued over whether converts should be required to follow Jewish law. Reformers Wycliffe and Hus were branded as heretics for insisting that people should be able to read the Bible in their own language. When Martin Luther took issue with the church's selling of indulgences, he launched one of the greatest debates of all time about Christian fundamentals, risking excommunication and even death for challenging accepted doctrine. Just a few years later, Protestants themselves systematically executed Anabaptists for holding to the "heresy" that a confession of faith should precede baptism. And in America, not so long ago, disagreements regarding the biblical view of slavery split denominations. The original Southern Baptist Convention organized, in part, because Baptists in the South did not want to be told by Baptists in the North that owning slaves is wrong. After all, they argued, the Bible clearly teaches that slaves should obey their masters.

Of course, in hindsight, it's easy to see where the church went wrong. In April of 1993, the pope formally acquitted Galileo of heresy, 360 years after his indictment. Similarly, the Southern Baptist Convention of 1995 voted to adopt a resolution renouncing its racist roots.

We would all like to believe that had we lived in the days of the early church or the Protestant Reformation, we would have chosen the side of truth, but in nearly every case, this would have required a deep questioning of the fundamental teachings of the time. It would have required a willingness to change. We must be wary of imitating the Pharisees, who bragged that had *they* lived during the time of the prophets, they would have protected the innocent (scc Matt. 23:30), but who then plotted against Jesus and persecuted his disciples.

With this in mind, I sometimes wonder what sort of convictions I might have held had I lived in a different time and place. Would I have used the Bible to defend my right to own slaves? Would I have cheered on the Crusades? Would I have chosen to follow Jesus in the first place?

This is why I try to keep an open mind about the monkeys, and it's why I consider myself an evolutionist — not necessarily of the scientific variety but of the faith variety. Just as living organisms are said to evolve over time, so faith evolves, on both a personal and a collective level. Spiritual evolution explains why Christianity has thrived while other ancient religions have perished. It explains why our brothers and sisters in rural Zimbabwe and those in the Greek Orthodox Church can worship the same God but in much different ways. Christianity never could have survived the ebb and flow of time, much less its own worldwide expansion, had God not created it with the innate ability to adapt to changing environments. The same versatility that allowed Paul to become all things to all people applies to the church collectively. The ability of the body of Christ to change — to grow fins when it needs to swim and wings when it needs to fly — has preserved it for over two thousand years, despite countless predictions of its imminent demise.

That's why I'm an evolutionist. I'm an evolutionist because I believe that the best way to reclaim the gospel in times of change is not to cling more tightly to our convictions but to hold them with an open hand. I'm an evolutionist because I believe that sometimes God uses changes in the environment to pry idols from our grip and teach us something new. But most of all, I'm an evolutionist because my own story is one of unlikely survival. If it hadn't been for evolution, I might have lost my faith.

It started small — a nagging question here, a new idea there, an ever-changing, freshly accessible world everywhere — but before I knew it, just as I was preparing to graduate from a Christian college ready to take the world for Jesus, twenty years of unquestioned assumptions about my faith were suddenly thrown into doubt.

No longer satisfied with easy answers, I started asking harder questions. I questioned what I thought were fundamentals — the eternal damnation of all non-Christians, the scientific and historical accuracy of the Bible, the ability to know absolute truth, and the politicization of evangelicalism. I questioned God: his fairness, regarding salvation; his goodness, for allowing poverty and injustice in the world; and his intelligence, for entrusting Christians to fix things. I wrestled with passages of Scripture that seemed to condone genocide and the oppression of women and struggled to make sense of the pride and hypocrisy within the church. I wondered if the God of my childhood was really the kind of God I wanted to worship, and at times I wondered if he even exists at all.

But rather than killing off my faith, these doubts led to a surprising rebirth. To survive in a new, volatile environment, I had to shed old convictions and grow new ones in their place. I had to take a closer look at what I believed and figure out what was truly essential. I went from the security of crawling around on all fours in the muck and mire of my inherited beliefs to the vulnerability of standing, my head and heart exposed, in the truth of my own spiritual experience. I evolved, not into a better creature than those around me but into a better, more adapted me — a me who wasn't afraid of her own ideas and doubts and intuitions, a me whose faith could survive change.

While evolution on a broad, historical scale happens every now and then, evolution within the souls of individuals happens every day, whenever we adapt our faith to change. Evolution means letting go of our false fundamentals so that God can get into those shadowy places we're not sure we want him to be. It means being okay with being wrong, okay with not having all the answers, okay with never being finished.

My story is about that kind of evolution. It's about moving from certainty, through doubt, to faith. It's not about the answers I found but about the questions I asked, questions I suspect you might be asking too. It's not a pretty story, or even a finished story. It's a survival story. It's the story of how I evolved in an unlikely environment, a little place called Monkey Town.

PART 1

HABITAT

CHAPTER 1

The Best Christian
Attitude Award

People sometimes ask me when I became a Christian, and that's a hard question to answer because I'm pretty sure that by the time I asked Jesus into my heart, he'd already been living there for a while. I was just five years old at the time, a compact little person with pigtails sticking out of my head like corn tassels, and I remember thinking it strange that someone as important as Jesus would need an invitation. Strange now is the fact that before I lost my first tooth or learned to ride a bike or graduated from kindergarten, I committed my life to a man who asked his followers to love their enemies, to give without expecting anything in return, and to face public execution if necessary. It is perhaps an unfair thing to ask of a child, but few who decide to follow Jesus know from the beginning what they're getting themselves into.

I cannot remember a time when I didn't know about Jesus. Stories of his dividing the fishes and loaves, calming the stormy sea, and riding the donkey into Jerusalem were as familiar to me growing up as *Jack and the Beanstalk* and *Cinderella*. I learned them from my parents and from pretty Sunday school teachers who smelled like peppermint and let me call them by their first names. They were more than stories really. They were grand narratives that flowed like streams into my own story, creating the currents that would move me forward and give me direction in life.

I had a simple but enviable childhood. We lived in Birmingham, Alabama, until I was twelve, in a small house with a big back yard that sat atop a hill overlooking the airport. A giant oak in the middle of the back yard shaded us in the summer and dropped shining amber leaves every autumn. During the day, my little sister, Amanda, and I gathered acorns and set shoebox traps for rabbits. At night, we sat on the front porch and watched the lights of airplanes rise and fall like wandering stars. For all we knew, we were rich as queens. The only time I suspected otherwise was when I overheard a friend of my mother teasing her about how she washed and reused plastic cups. Apparently we were poor, but not *that* poor.

The daughter of a genuine, certified theologian, I'd memorized the "Four Spiritual Laws" before I'd memorized my own address. My father earned a graduate degree from Dallas Theological Seminary, a school famous for producing megachurch pastors like Chuck Swindoll, Tony Evans, and Andy Stanley. Instead of pursuing full-time ministry, however, my father committed his life to Christian education, which I suppose explains the plastic cups. A college professor, he often invited his brightest students over for coffee and long talks about hermeneutics and eschatology and epistemology. I loved falling asleep to the sound of their voices undulating from the living room. I felt secure in knowing that while I slept, my father was awake having important conversations about God.

I always looked up to my father with a sense of reverent awe. It wasn't that I thought he possessed supernatural powers or anything; I just imagined that he and God had a lot of things in common, that they subscribed to the same magazines and wore similar shoes. Looking back, I realize how important it was that my father loved me so openly and listened so carefully. My first impressions of my heavenly Father were that he too was gentle, playful, and kind.

Despite knowing about dispensationalism long before I probably should have, I never felt trapped in a world of endless churchgoing. My mother had been raised Independent Baptist and as a girl was forbidden to dance and go to movies. Determined to avoid legalism, she let Amanda and me wait until we were good and ready before we got baptized, took communion, or asked Jesus into our hearts. Her private disdain for potlucks and church business meetings kept us from being at church every time the doors were opened, and I noticed that she got a little fidgety whenever the pastor discussed wives submitting to their husbands. I loved this about her, the same way I loved the scent of her cherry-almond lotion when she tucked me into bed at night.

A substitute teacher at my elementary school, my mother earned a reputation for doting on the needy kids. Those with absent parents, stained shirts, runny noses, and learning disabilities always left her classroom beaming with self-confidence.

I think I must have gotten my bleeding heart from her, which, combined with my father's cautious idealism, accidentally made me into a liberal. If my father gave Christianity a head, my mother gave it a heart and hands, and it was her tender telling of the story of the cross, mingled with cherry almond, that first moved me to ask Jesus into my heart.

When you're a kid, being a Christian is like being part of a secret society. I remember getting all excited whenever I spotted one of those silver *ichthus* emblems on someone's car or heard Amy Grant music playing in the background at the grocery store. Nothing thrilled me more than identifying fellow believers, especially famous ones. "Did you hear that Donnie from New Kids on the Block got saved?" my best friend, Julie, asked as we gathered acorns from under the oak tree. "My dad says Michael Jordan is a Christian," I added. It meant that they were one of us, that they too knew the secret password for getting into heaven. I'll admit I was a little disappointed when I learned that something like 85 percent of Americans identify themselves as Christians. Knowing you're in the majority makes the whole thing a lot less dramatic and sexy.

The culture wars of the 1980s and '90s raged throughout my most formative years, culminating with the election of George W. Bush my sophomore year of college. In this political environment, being a good Christian meant adopting a range of causes, such as protecting the traditional family, keeping God in the Pledge of Allegiance, and supporting the right to bear arms. I knew what abortion was before I knew where babies come from, and I learned how to effectively blame everything from crime rates to suicide rates on the removal of prayer from public schools. I cried for hours when I learned that my paternal grandfather, a lifelong Democrat, supported Bill Clinton in 1996; I was under the impression this meant Grandpa would go to hell.

An evangelical in the truest sense of the word, I once wrote the plan of salvation on a piece of construction paper, folded it into a paper airplane, and sent it soaring over the fence into the back yard of our Mormon neighbors. Amanda tattled on me, so I spent the rest of the afternoon on my belly in the dirt, trying to drag it back under the fence with a stick. I saw my neighborhood as my first mission field, often coaxing Amanda and Julie into going along with some crazy evangelistic scheme like sticking tracts in people's mailboxes or singing hymns at the top of our lungs as we rode our bikes down the street. According to Julie, once when I spent the night at her house, the dryer buzzer startled me so badly that I jumped out of my bed and announced that Jesus had returned to rapture us all.

I guess when you grow up listening to Ravi Zacharias on your way to kindergarten in the morning, you kind of turn into a Jesus freak. I was the nutcase kid who removed wise men figurines from manger scenes at Christmas to more accurately depict the historical time line of Advent. I gently corrected my Sunday school teacher when she referred to Jonah getting swallowed up by the *whale* (everyone knows that the word is literally translated "big fish") or referenced the forbidden *apple* in the garden of Eden (which was more likely some sort of Middle Eastern fruit, like a fig). My mother reminded me almost daily that my primary responsibility in life was to go to a good Christian college and marry a good Christian boy. I guess I just assumed that I would stay a Christian forever. It was like being an American — not something you could just go and change.

By the time I reached fourth grade, I knew so much about defending the existence of God that I used the same apologetic strategies to defend the existence of Santa Claus to my increasingly skeptical classmates. Our conversations on the playground usually went something like this:

Skeptic: How do you know that Santa is real? Have you ever seen him?

Me: No, I haven't. But Santa leaves enough evidence of his existence to prove it beyond a reasonable doubt. Every year I find presents from him under the tree and little crumbs all over the kitchen table where I left his plate of cookies. I might not see Santa himself, but these things point to him, as bending trees point to the existence of wind.

Skeptic: How come there's a different Santa in every department store?

Me: Those are Santa's helpers, who, with his permission, disguise themselves as Mr. Claus in order to more efficiently compile a list of what the children across the world want for Christmas.

Skeptic: Everyone knows that reindeer can't fly. How does Santa get around?

Me: Yes, it is true that most reindeer cannot fly. However, reindeer empowered by the Holy Spirit can do anything God tells them to do, and those are the kind of reindeer Santa owns. For a prototype, read the story of Balaam's donkey in the book of Numbers.

Skeptic: How can one person make it to every rooftop in the world in just one night?

Me: Who says Santa is a person? Although Saint Nick is not mentioned by name, the Bible clearly points to the existence of supernatural angelic beings whose primary directive is to protect, inform, and bless humans. If Santa is an angel on a mission from God to reward the good children of the world, he's likely to boast supernatural strength and speed.

Skeptic: What about those kids who say they saw their parents sneaking presents under the tree on Christmas Eve?

Me: Unfortunately, these kids may be telling the truth. You see, the scope of Santa's power in our lives is ultimately dependent upon our willingness to accept it. Parents who choose not to believe in Santa forfeit the blessing of his visits forever, and so they must rely on their own methods for supplying kids with presents at Christmas.

Skeptic: Why do bad kids still get presents?

Me: Why, grace, of course.

I could have written a book called *When Skeptics Ask: A Handbook on Yuletide Evidences*, but of course, after a long and gruesome internal battle, I eventually gave the thing up. I suppose the realization came gradually, as I grew old enough to recognize the playful nuances in the voices of adults when they asked what Santa had brought me for Christmas and the puzzling inconsistencies in how he distributed gifts. It also occurred to me that if Santa were in fact real, my favorite apologist, Josh McDowell, would be using him as evidence of the supernatural.

As a child, the only time I ever doubted God was when my skin flared up. For most of my life, I suffered from such severe eczema that the slightest trigger sent my body into full-out rebellion against itself. All it took was a tiny piece of walnut hidden in a brownie, a stressful week at school, a polyester jacket, or some mysterious unknown allergen, and I'd break out in itchy rashes that had me tearing into my arms and legs for days. I'd scratch until I bled, leaving long red gashes in my skin that could get infected and turn into open sores or boils. Ashamed of what I had done to myself, I hid under long sleeves and pants, and cowered in the corners of the locker room before gym class. I kept a crinkled tube of hydrocortisone with me at all times. I cut my fingernails down to the quick and wore socks over my hands at night.

My eczema added an element of frenzy to everything I did. Home videos show me opening my birthday presents and scratching, reading to Amanda and scratching, sitting on Santa's lap and scratching, looking at Mount Rushmore and scratching. I was all elbows and movement, like Animal in a Muppets special. My parents took me to every dermatologist in Birmingham, each with his own ridiculous home remedy. One routine involved lathering me with petroleum jelly and then rolling me up in bath towels like a mummy for thirty minutes. Another had me bathing in a pungent mixture of lukewarm water and vinegar three times a week. When things got really bad, my mother would relent and let the doctor give me a steroid shot. For a few days after, I enjoyed skin as soft as a baby's.

"You might grow out of it, you know," one doctor told me. "My daughter had severe eczema until she was twelve. She just woke up one morning and it was gone." The doctor's anecdote gave me a goal on which to focus. Every night I scratched and I prayed for God to make me grow out of my skin.

All kids have their paranoias. Amanda went a month without eating solid foods because she was convinced that her throat was closing up, and Julie spent weeks searching for her real parents after reading *The Face on the Milk Carton*. Growing up, my greatest fear was that I would find God out, that I would accidentally stumble upon some terrible, unspeakable thing that proved he wasn't as great and good as grown-ups made him out to be. Sometimes when I woke up to find my sheets stained with blood, I wondered if God was even listening or if he was busy doing something else. Sometimes I wondered if he even exists at all. All the amorphous misgivings and perplexities that crept around my little subconscious began to take the shape of one nagging question: What if I'm wrong?

It wasn't enough to undo my young faith, but the question stayed with me, like a rock in my shoe.

I'm not sure why—perhaps because I wanted to impress my father, perhaps because I thought it might catch God's attention —but as a kid, I obsessed over winning awards. From AWANA badges, to gymnastics ribbons, to marching-band trophies, my room glittered with the spoils of overachievement. Of particular pride to me were awards that honored my religious aptitude, the crown jewel of which was the coveted Best Christian Attitude Award.

I attended a private elementary school in Birmingham, where just about all of my classmates were Christians, a fact that had little effect on our behavior, of course, except that being Christians meant that if we were in trouble with the teacher, we were also in trouble with God. Each year just two students from each class, one girl and one boy, received the Best Christian Attitude Award. It was the only award for which the students actually voted, making it a sort of spiritualized popularity contest that even awkward noncheerleaders like myself had a chance at winning.

My strategy for winning the Best Christian Attitude Award each year included keeping extra pens and pencils in my desk to loan to needy students, graciously allowing my classmates to cut in front of me in line at the water fountain, trying not to tattle in an effort to secure the troublemaker vote, and writing sweet notes of encouragement to Isabella and Juanita, to procure the swing minority vote.

During the daily prayer-request time, I made a point of addressing the plight of the poor, homeless, and heathen, while all the other kids droned on and on about their sick hamsters. I toted my Bible around, even to gym class, and took every opportunity to casually mention that my father was a theologian. If I sensed a threat (like in fifth grade, when everyone knew that Christina Simpson wanted to be a missionary when she grew up), I shrewdly reserved all of my tattling for her so that at the end of the year she had a few more demerits than I did. I was remarkably calculating and conniving for my age — starting rumors about the competition, sweeping in to befriend new students, acting especially innocent and saccharine in the weeks leading up to the vote. I suspect I was the only kid in the entire school who thought year-round about the Best Christian Attitude Award.

I won the Best Christian Attitude Award four years in a row and probably would have won it again if I hadn't transferred to a public school in eighth grade, where its existence would violate the establishment clause of the First Amendment. I've always felt that awards have a way of calling an internal truce between my secret hope of being "discovered" and my persistent fear of being "found out." Getting an award means people still suspect that I'm an exceptionally wonderful and talented person. It means they have no idea that beneath it all, I'm a complete fraud. Awards delay the inevitable.

I remember thinking about this in sixth grade, just minutes after the ballots were collected for the Best Christian Attitude Award. I was worrying about whether the teacher could deduce from my handwriting that I had voted for myself, when Evan, the chubby sandy-haired boy who sat to my right, accidently dropped his pencil. It rolled across the aisle and stopped under my desk. Evan silently signaled for me to please pick it up for him, and I hesitated because he was a troublemaker, and I didn't want the teacher to catch me passing things back and forth with a troublemaker. It crossed my mind that helping him out would earn me some Best Christian Attitude Award points, but then I remembered that we had already taken the vote, so I just smiled back at him, shrugged my shoulders, and hoped he wouldn't end up in my class next year. Poor Evan lumbered away from his desk to pick up his pencil, which resulted in a severe scolding from the teacher (who for some reason really hated it when kids left their desks), earning him double demerits. I'll never forget the look of dismay and betrayal on his face and the way my heart sank like a stone when I saw it.

It reminded me of this time when Amanda and I were playing in the woods behind our house, and we noticed a little confluence of blue butterflies around what appeared to be a shiny black rock. We marveled at their brilliant sapphire wings, but when I moved in to get a closer look, I discovered that the shiny black rock wasn't a rock at all but rather a dead rat snake, upon whose carcass the butterflies were feeding. My skin tingled, and a thick wave of dread and fear rushed through my body. Not wanting to freak Amanda out, I challenged her to a race back to the house. As we ran through the trees and down the hill, I felt as though I carried some sort of heavy, unspeakable secret. For some reason, I decided that I couldn't tell anybody about what I'd seen, not even my parents. The scene was just too rotten, too disturbing. To this day, I never see one of those blue butterflies without getting this strange, unexplainable sense of foreboding.

I think every person remembers the first time they were confronted with their own depravity. Mine was when I refused to pick up Evan's pencil. That was when I realized I was a sinner, no better than the soldiers who crucified Jesus on the cross. The terrible, unspeakable thing I was afraid of finding in God I had found in myself. I felt like an imposter, like a dirty secret. I was a brilliant sapphire butterfly feeding off the remains of a dead snake.

When I was thirteen, my family moved from Birmingham to the town of Dayton, Tennessee, home of the famous Scopes Monkey Trial of 1925. My father took an administrative position at Bryan College, a small Christian university in town, named in honor of William Jennings Bryan, famed defender of creationism. The school was enjoying an uptick in enrollment, thanks in part to warnings from evangelical leaders about the dangers of a secular education, and among the perks was free tuition for Amanda and me. Bryan's sprawling campus sat atop one of Dayton's highest points, so faculty and students referred to it as "the city on a hill." From the chapel, you could look down into the valley and see the entire town — its famous courthouse, the city hall, the bright lights of the Dayton City School football stadium, a smokestack sending puffs of steam curling toward the sky.

In one of my first letters to Julie, I wrote that "everyone in this town is a Christian," trying not to betray my dismay at having no one to evangelize anymore. Indeed, the Bible Belt culture permeated every part of life in Dayton, from lengthy prayers held at the openings of beauty pageants and city council meetings, to laws that forbade the sale of liquor by the drink, to the little brick churches positioned on nearly every street corner.

Most of my science teachers skipped the chapters on evolution in our biology textbooks, fearing a backlash from parents.

With this in mind, my parents felt comfortable enough enrolling me in the public high school in the fall of 1995, where devotions were held over the intercom every morning and where each Rhea County High School football game began with prayer. (Apparently, nobody in Dayton got the memo from Madalyn Murray O'Hair.) I went to school with the same kids who went to my church, so I found my place in a clique of religious band nerds who introduced me to the entertainment staples of rural life: bonfires in the spring, skinny-dipping in the summer, toilet-papering yards in the fall, and bowling in the winter.

For the most part, my life in high school revolved around youth-group activities and the practice schedule of the Rhea County High School Golden Eagle Marching Band. I played the flute during concert season and the piccolo during football season. Sometimes when I found the music particularly challenging or the marching strenuous, I faked it. My best friend, Sarah, chauffeured me around town in her little red hatchback, making sure we got everywhere on time — Bible Club, youth group, band camp, Friday-night football games. Funny and sensible, Sarah not only tolerated my religious zeal but seemed to admire it. She helped me plan Bible Club meetings and See You at the Pole, meticulously taking care of all the details while I did the flashier stuff, like leading prayers and giving speeches. I thanked her by making dozens of mixtapes. Choppy composites of my musical obsessions at the time, they represented the cacophony of voices that helped define our shared high school experience: Pearl Jam, Rich Mullins, John Philip Sousa.

I felt closer to God as a teenager than at any other time in my life. I prayed incessantly, casting all the insecurities of adolescence at the feet of my heavenly Father, who loved me better than any boy ever could and who looked past my braces and bangs to see his beautiful, unblemished child. The Bible read like poetry to me, each word and verse ripe with spiritual sustenance. It fed me, and I swallowed without asking questions or entertaining doubts or choking on the bones. Sometimes I took the wooded path from my back yard to the Bryan College campus, where I sat under a sprawling white oak—much like the one from my childhood—and meditated on Scripture. I half expected to lift up my eyes and see Jesus perched on one of the highest boughs, smiling down at me as I prayed. He never seemed farther away than the corner of my eye.

So with Jesus watching over my shoulder and with the best of intentions, I devoted myself to witnessing to my Rhea County High School classmates. This proved to be a bit of a challenge since most of them were already Christians. My strategy was to be effusively friendly to everyone I met, always looking for openings in the conversation that would naturally lead to a discussion about substitutionary atonement. At lunch and between classes, I chatted it up with just about anyone who would listen, from the sulky cheerleaders who didn't know my name, to the Goths hiding behind layers of makeup, to the good ol' boys whose camouflage jackets smelled of dry leaves and cigarettes. The way I saw it, the problem in Dayton wasn't that people hadn't heard about Christianity; it was that Christianity was so infused in the culture of Dayton, it served as a kind of folk religion. Nearly everyone I met had responded to an altar call at one point or another. So I became more convinced than ever that the best, most secure Christians were those who knew what they believed and why they believed it. Salvation wasn't just about being a Christian; it was about being the right kind of Christian, the kind who did things by the Book.

I directed my efforts toward evangelizing the evangelized, launching morning Bible studies and prayer walks, inviting people to church, and handing out free copies of *The Case for Christ*. I wrote an inspirational column in the student newspaper and worked my Christian worldview into essays and creative writing projects whenever possible. Just in case anyone doubted where I stood, I took a magic marker and wrote "God Is Awesome" on a piece of red duct tape and stuck it to my backpack.

Really, it's a testament to the power of teenage hormones that anyone wanted to date me at all. A poster child for the True Love Waits movement, at sixteen I was quoted in a *Christianity Today* article highlighting the federally funded abstinence-education program at my school. "By the end of the class," I told the reporter, "people who were sexually active felt so dumb, they didn't tell anybody. Now I can hold my head up high. Yeah, I'm a virgin."

I may have been the only teenager on the planet who enjoyed guilt-based purity lessons more than the adults giving them, and yet I managed to attract a few boys who thought that an excessively friendly, large-breasted girl with a purity ring and a savior complex sounded intriguing, especially the year *Cruel Intentions* was released. The smartest ones feigned interest in talking about spirituality so that they could get my phone number. Few made it past the first two-hour diatribe about being equally yoked.

Sarah and I spent hours talking about how much easier it would be once we got to Bryan College, where every guy wanted to get married and go to seminary. We imagined that there we would find likeminded friends, answers to all of our questions about God, and husbands who would whisk us away from Dayton to some exotic location, like the mission field or a megachurch.

Sometimes I long for the days when I was so certain, when faith was as sure a thing as thunder after a lightning flash or the scent of almond cherry at night. Things have changed a lot since then, but not necessarily for the worst.

CHAPTER 2

June the
Ten Commandments Lady

The first time I ever saw the Ten Commandments Lady in person, she was singing "Amazing Grace" next to the napkin dispenser at McDonald's. It was a chilly Thursday night in late November, and as usual, there was standing room only at the weekly gospel-music singing attended by hundreds of old-timers from Dayton. It took me until the third stanza — "Through many dangers, toils, and snares" — to recognize June as the soloist. She appeared so put-together, with her thick, gray hair pulled tightly away from her face and her thin frame poised politely in front of the microphone. She wore an apple-red suit with a miniature Ten Commandments tablet on the lapel, and her soprano voice carried the tune well. Could this thin, unassuming sixtysomething be June Griffin, legendary defender of the Ten Commandments, the Bill of Rights, and biblical authority? The hesitant applause that followed her performance told me I'd indeed found her. Nobody in this town has ever really known what to make of June Griffin.

June, who lives by the motto "For God and country," has lived in the area for more than twenty years now. Before that night, I'd seen her picture in the paper many times. She ran several unsuccessful campaigns for Congress on the platform of eliminating income tax, Social Security, and welfare. She is the founder of Citizen Soldiers for the Atomic Bomb, a group that confronts any antinuclear protests at the nearby Oak Ridge National Laboratory and "prays for the untimely death" of those opposed to America's right to defend herself against her enemies.

The first I ever heard of June was in high school, back in the late nineties, when my school bus went by her general store on Highway 27 every morning and afternoon. Outside the store she kept a marquee-style sign that generated all kinds of controversy when she rearranged the letters each week, making statements like "Sexual Immorality Leads to Eternal Punishment" during the Clinton-Lewinsky scandal, "AIDS Is a Curse from God" on World AIDS day, and "Nice Shot" on Martin Luther King Jr. Day. On graduation morning in 1999, she posted a message warning me and my fellow high school graduates that "Higher Education = Moral Degradation."

June earned her name as the Ten Commandments Lady when, in response to Alabama's banishment of Judge Roy Moore and his famous Ten Commandments monument in 2003, she traveled to all ninety-five Tennessee counties to try to convince elected officials to display the Decalogue in public buildings. Thanks to June, the 5,280-pound granite monument that they kicked out of Alabama made a stop in Dayton in the back of a flatbed truck before it embarked on a nationwide tour. In her crusade to save the Ten Commandments, June has written hundreds of letters to newspapers across the state. She wrote so many to the local paper that the editor of the *Dayton Herald* had to place a limit on how many letters an individual could submit in a given week. If you Google June's name, you will encounter hundreds of her essays, which range in subject from a case for the divinity of Christ to a tribute to white supremacist Byron De La Beckwith. On the side, June makes extra money selling her frilly "Bill of Rights" apron at conventions and fairs. It includes two pockets: one for your Bible and one for your gun.

June's most recent campaign has been against what she sees as the invasion of our country by foreigners. June got herself arrested recently when she stormed into a Mexican store downtown, demanding that the owner, a legal immigrant, remove the Mexican flag from his store window. When he refused, she tore it down and demanded that he "learn to speak English or get out." The store owner contacted police, who charged June with theft, vandalism, and civil rights intimidation. When one local reporter keenly asked June if "Thou shalt not steal" wasn't one of the Ten Commandments, she insisted that God would let her off the hook on this one since her actions were part of a righteous war. She waved a "Remember the Alamo" banner on her way to the Rhea County Jail.

I thought about all of this as I listened to June sing under the golden arches that night about being in heaven for ten thousand years, "bright shining as the sun." When the hymn concluded, she closed her eyes and said, "Thank you, Jesus," which was followed by an obligatory "amen" from a smattering of seniors in the crowd. As I stood there next to a cardboard cutout of Ronald

McDonald, I wondered for a moment what on earth God does with people like June when it comes time for judgment. She's certainly not the only one who professes the name of Jesus Christ in one breath and then curses her neighbor in the next. Is that profession enough to save her? Is it worth more to God than the faith of a Buddhist or Hindu or Muslim who practices kindness and compassion?

Like a lot of people, I tend to assume that God will judge people the way I judge people; so I decided that God would probably just give June a good talking-to come judgment day. I figured he'd embarrass her in front of everybody, sort of put her in her place, before forgiving her and then welcoming her into the kingdom. I imagined that this would happen about the same time he explained to the religious right that he wasn't a Republican, to John Calvin that he didn't predetermine his salvation, and to Andrew Jackson that he was insulted by the notion of Manifest Destiny. Judgment day, I imagined, would be one big embarrassment for those who got it wrong and one big vindication for those of us who got it right.

Only after a few minutes did it occur to me that this might not necessarily work out to my advantage.

I was at McDonald's that night to work on a feel-good freelance article for a Christian senior citizens' magazine, so I snapped a picture of June, as I had all the other soloists, just to be polite. Of course, I had no intention of giving the Ten Commandments Lady any more press than she needed. But before I could leave, June pulled me aside to ask what I was working on. I told her that the story was for a Methodist publishing company, which disgusted her enough to abandon the subject, since she has created her own denomination and has no use for any others, particularly liberal ones. But before I could leave, she grabbed my arm and pointed to a mustached man sitting near the PA system.

"You should take a picture of him," she prodded. "Don't you think he looks just like the great Jeff Davis himself?"

"Maybe later," I said, eager to escape the gaze of her piercing hazel eyes.

It took me two days to figure out that she was referring to Jefferson Davis, president of the Southern Confederacy.

CHAPTER 3

Monkey Town

Two months ago the town was obscure and happy.
Today it is a universal joke.

— H. L. MENCKEN, *BALTIMORE EVENING SUN*, JULY 9, 1925

Some say it was Moses' fault for not asking for more details when God told him about creating the heavens and the earth. Others say it was Darwin's fault for writing *The Origin of the Species*. Some blame the media, others blame the legal system, but most folks in Dayton, Tennessee, have pretty well settled on the fact that it was George Rappleyea's fault that our city will forever be known as Monkey Town.

The whole thing started back in May of 1925, when Rappleyea rushed into Robinson's Drugstore with a plan to "put Dayton on the map." A New York native with a thick Yankee accent, horn-rimmed glasses, and a head full of modern ideas, Rappleyea was a bit of an alien in this tiny conservative town in East Tennessee, but most folks liked him. That fateful morning, he managed to capture the attention of some of the town's most influential citizens, who, in the days of Prohibition, liked to gather around the soda fountain at Robinson's to discuss business. "Mr. Robinson, you and John Godfrey are always looking for something that will get Dayton a little publicity," Rappleyea reportedly said. "I wonder if you have seen the morning paper?"[2] Rappleyea, who managed the struggling coal-mining business in the area, had discovered an advertisement in the *Chattanooga Times* from the American Civil Liberties Union offering to support any Tennessee schoolteacher willing to challenge the state's new antievolution laws, which forbade the teaching of evolution in public schools. The evolution-creationism debate had taken center stage in recent years, and it didn't take long for Rappleyea to convince Mr. Robinson and the rest of the drugstore regulars that hosting such a controversial test trial would reap economic benefits for the town of Dayton.

The group decided to call in local schoolteacher John T. Scopes, who they hoped would volunteer as the defendant in the case. Scopes, a quiet and unassuming man, admitted that he may have taught evolution in a biology class at the local high school and, more for idealistic reasons than capitalistic ones, agreed to serve as the defendant in the trial. Local attorney Sue Hicks, a man named after his late mother, agreed to coordinate the prosecution with the assistance of his brother, Herbert. (If this part of the story sounds familiar, it's because Sue Hicks served as the inspiration for Johnny Cash's "A Boy Named Sue.") With prosecutors and a defendant in place, the Robinson's Drugstore gang had pieced together the publicity stunt they were looking for.

Luckily for them, the trial attracted some bigger names than the Boy Named Sue. Clarence Darrow, a famous criminal defense lawyer and an outspoken agnostic, volunteered his services for the defense, and William Jennings Bryan, a fundamentalist politician and "the Great Commoner," volunteered his services for the prosecution. With these two ideological heavyweights in the ring, the Scopes trial was billed as a showdown between science and religion, "the trial of the century."

More than two hundred reporters, from as far away as London, descended on Dayton during that hot summer of 1925. For the first time in history, a radio station broadcast the court proceedings live. Pictures of grinning monkeys sipping soda and holding medicine jars adorned billboards and shop windows across town, and Robinson's Drugstore proudly displayed a banner proclaiming "Where It All Started." Protestors, activists, and preachers made pilgrimages to Dayton, so residents erected a giant platform on the courthouse lawn to accommodate any impromptu lectures or debates. (It was rumored that George Rappleyea actually staged a fistfight there.) People could pay to get their picture made with a live chimpanzee, and the town constable even put a sign on his motorcycle that read "Monkeyville Police." A *New York Times* reporter wrote that "whatever the deep significance of the trial, if it has any, there is no doubt that it has attracted some of the world's champion freaks."[3]

However, both Darrow and Bryan believed the trial to be of much more significance than just another Roaring Twenties sideshow. The two men had spent their entire lives promoting opposing ideologies, and the trial presented them with an opportunity to bring national attention to their causes. Bryan was sixty-five at the time and had not practiced law in thirty years, but that didn't matter to the people of Dayton, who knew him as a great orator and champion of Christian fundamentalism. A three-time Democratic Party nominee for president, Bryan spent his political career fighting on behalf of progressive causes like labor rights and women's suffrage and against imperialism, alcohol, and Darwinism. Known as "the Great Commoner," he prided himself in representing the interests of regular people. He served in Congress and as Secretary of State for Woodrow Wilson, resigning from the cabinet in protest of the US involvement in World War I. For Bryan, the theory of evolution, particularly social Darwinism, represented a devastating threat to the moral and biblical foundation of American society, a threat that endangered all the things he had worked his whole life to preserve.

Darrow, sixty-eight, did not share the same popularity among Dayton residents. A leading member of the American Civil Liberties Union, Darrow was best known for using insanity pleas and existential philosophy to save his clients from the death penalty, or to "let them off the hook," some liked to say. He fought for individual liberty, freedom of speech, and educators' right to teach the theory of evolution. He saw Tennessee's antievolution laws as an unconstitutional and backward attempt by biblical absolutists to keep modernity at bay. The odds were against him in this case, considering the fundamentalist attitude of the local population and of the jury. During the trial, Darrow expressed dismay at the giant "Read Your Bible" sign draped across the courthouse door. However, the press remained sympathetic to his cause, which gave him an important ally.

When the trial finally began, there was standing room only in our famous little courthouse. It can get pretty hot here in July, so all the old, yellowed film footage of the Scopes trial shows participants fanning their faces vigorously and wiping their brows with handkerchiefs. The defense immediately attempted to quash the indictment against Scopes on state and federal constitutional grounds, but the judge denied their motion. So the trial, which would likely end in Scopes' prosecution, simply became an excuse for Bryan and Darrow to launch attacks on one another whenever the opportunity presented itself. In their opening statements, both men lectured on the momentous nature of the case and the great struggle between science and religion. At one point, a debate erupted over whether to allow a biologist to testify for the defense, resulting in cheers and boos from observers. In between all of the rhetoric, a few high school students were called to testify about Scopes' teaching of evolution at Rhea County High School.

The trial reached a climax when, on the seventh day of proceedings, the defense called William Jennings Bryan himself to the stand as an expert on the Bible. By this time, the trial had been moved to the courthouse lawn to better accommodate the swarms of spectators and press, so thousands watched as Bryan and Darrow finally got the chance to go head-to-head in the trial of the century.

Darrow, who had by this point removed his coat and tie, immediately began grilling Bryan with questions designed to undermine a literalist interpretation of the Bible. Darrow questioned his opponent on everything from the creation account of Genesis to the story of Jonah and the whale (which Bryan rightly noted was actually the story of Jonah and the big fish). At first Bryan appeared confident, answering as slowly and methodically as the wave of his palm-frond fan. However, as the questioning went on, his lack of preparation became obvious.

"The Bible says Joshua commanded the sun to stand still for the purpose of lengthening the day, doesn't it, and you believe it?" Darrow pressed.

"I do."

"Do you believe at that time the entire sun went around the earth?"

"No, I believe that the earth goes around the sun."

"Do you believe that the men who wrote it thought that the day could be lengthened or that the sun could be stopped?"

"I don't know what they thought."

"You don't know?" Darrow asked with mock surprise.

"I think they wrote the fact without expressing their own thoughts," Bryan returned.

At this point, the attorney general interrupted the proceedings to tell the judge that he thought the line of questioning was irrelevant to the case. However, Judge Raulston, who seemed to be enjoying himself, said that if Mr. Bryan was willing to be examined, he saw no reason why the two should stop.

Darrow asked a few more questions, paced back and forth across the stage, and returned to the subject of Joshua and the sun.

"Now, Mr. Bryan, have you ever pondered what would have happened to the earth if it had stood still?"

"No."

"You have not?"

"No, sir. The God I believe in could have taken care of that, Mr. Darrow."

"I see. Have you ever pondered what would naturally happen to the earth if it stood still suddenly?"

"No."

"Don't you know it would have been converted into a molten mass of matter?"

"You testify to that when you get on the stand," Bryan shot back. "I will give you a chance."

"Don't you believe it?" Darrow asked.

"I would want to hear expert testimony on that."

"You have never investigated that subject?"

"I don't think I have ever had the question asked."

"Or ever thought of it?"

"I have been too busy on things that I thought were of more importance than that," said Bryan.

Darrow went on to challenge Bryan about the age of the earth and the biblical account of the worldwide flood.

"When was the flood?" he asked.

"I wouldn't attempt to fix the date," said Bryan.

"About 4004 BC?"

"That has been the estimate of a [biblical scholar] that is accepted today. I would not say it is accurate," Bryan responded cautiously.

"But what do you think the Bible itself says?" Darrow pressed. "Do you know how that estimate was arrived at?"

"I never made a calculation."

"A calculation from what?"

"I could not say."

"From the generations of man?"

"I would not want to say that."

"What do you think?" Darrow pushed.

"I do not think about things I don't think about," said Bryan.

"Do you think about things you do think about?" Darrow asked slyly, drawing laughter from the crowd.

As the questioning grew more heated, the prosecution tried repeatedly to pull Bryan off the stand, but he insisted on remaining.

"These gentlemen have not had much chance," Bryan said. "They did not come here to try this case. They came here to try revealed religion. I am here to defend it, and they can ask me any question they please."

The crowd, which some estimate had swelled to about three thousand, roared, and the judge allowed Darrow to continue to press Bryan with questions about the biblical time line.

"You have never in all your life made any attempt to find out about the other peoples of the earth," Darrow asked with feigned exasperation, "how old their civilizations are, how long they have existed on earth ..."

"No, sir," said Bryan. "I have been so well satisfied with the Christian religion that I have spent no time trying to find arguments against it."

"Were you afraid you might find some?" Darrow asked.

"I have all the information I want to live by and to die by," said Bryan.

To this Darrow charged, "And that's all you are interested in?"

"I am not looking for any more on religion."

"You don't care how old the earth is, how old man is, or how long the animals have been here?"

"I am not so much interested in that," said Bryan.

"You have never made any investigation to find out?"

"No, sir, I have never."

Finally, Bryan conceded that various interpretations of the creation account existed and that his understanding was that the days of creation represented periods of time rather than literal days, which led to a heated exchange.

"Have you any idea of the length of these periods?"

"No, I don't."

"Do you think the sun was made on the fourth day?"

"Yes."

"And they had evening and morning without the sun?"

"I am simply saying it is a period."

"They had evening and morning for four periods without the sun, do you think?"

Bryan's response was telling: "I believe in creation as there told, and if I am not able to explain it, I will accept it."

After nearly an hour of questioning, the judge finally got frustrated with the proceedings and adjourned the court. Supporters of both Bryan and Darrow declared victory, although it became clear the next day that the prosecution had no intention of putting Bryan on the witness stand again. The defense rested its case and suggested that the court instruct the jury to find the defendant guilty. This move deprived Bryan of the chance to question Darrow and to deliver a closing statement, and the trial soon came to an end. Scopes was found guilty and fined a hundred dollars.

Some have said that Bryan won the case, but Darrow won the argument.

Everybody left Dayton just as quickly as they came, and a few days later, after traveling around the area delivering speeches and sermons against secularism, Bryan died in his sleep during an afternoon nap. He died right here in Monkey Town.

Despite the ambitions of the Robinson's Drugstore gang, Dayton faded back into obscurity after the trial, and today it remains a small manufacturing town of about six thousand, nestled in the foothills of the Appalachians. The coal mines closed long ago and were replaced by factories, the largest of which belongs to La-Z-Boy Furniture, Dayton's biggest employer. The town grows in little fits and starts, but the countywide ban on selling liquor keeps a lot of potential chain restaurants at bay. A Super Walmart built at the south end of town a few years ago was welcomed like the second coming. My mother likes to refer to Dayton as "Little D," a wry allusion to Dallas, Texas, or "Big D," where she and my father lived while he was in seminary.

Cradled by the Tennessee River on its eastern border, Rhea

County is surrounded by three nuclear power plants, and you can see two of them from the top of Dayton Mountain on a clear day. These imposing landmarks are owned by the Tennessee Valley Authority, part of Roosevelt's New Deal and a ubiquitous presence in the eastern part of the state, where the TVA provides nine million residents with power. To control flooding, the TVA drains Chickamauga Lake every winter, leaving a swampy, desolate wound in the middle of Dayton for four months. The lake is so pristine and deep and green during the rest of the year that retirees build big houses all around it, and they spend their money in our grocery stores and bait shops.

Folks around here don't waste much time debating who really won the trial of the century. The bronze statue of William Jennings Bryan that stands guard on the courthouse lawn speaks for itself. The local newspaper lists more than one hundred churches in its directory, and every Thursday night McDonald's hosts a gospel-music singing for seniors. Signs announcing revivals and church picnics line the highway winding up Dayton Mountain. Neighbors look out for one another, and people always bring food when somebody dies. It's a community in the best sense of the word.

Largely unaffected by its historic past, Dayton moves at a slow, methodical pace. Conversation in the beauty salon changes with the seasons. We talk about who will be crowned Strawberry Queen at this year's Strawberry Festival, how the high school quarterback looks for the year, why the EPA won't let us fix the creeks that flood every spring, who's in charge of hanging the Christmas wreaths on the lampposts downtown.

Only every now and then do we have what I like to call "a Monkey Town moment," the most recent of which occurred when the Rhea County Commission voted to make homosexuality illegal in Dayton.

In March 2004, eight of our elected leaders passed a resolution calling for a ban on homosexuality and an amendment to state law that would allow the county to charge gay and lesbian people with crimes against nature. When word of the decision reached the press, it was as if the Scopes trial had come to Dayton all over again.

Within twenty-four hours, thousands of calls, from as far away as Australia, flooded the county offices. The local paper published four pages of letters to the editor. A group of Independent Baptists organized a march "for our American godly heritage" through the streets of downtown Dayton, and a local high school student coordinated a gay pride rally. The courthouse lawn was crowded with street preachers calling for the deportation of "sodomites," teenagers waving rainbow-striped flags, and of course, reporters from all over the country taking every opportunity to remind the world that this was, in fact, the same Monkey Town of 1925.

One preacher carried a cross up and down Highway 27 through Dayton for a week. Another hoisted into the bed of his Chevy an enormous sign that read "Sodomites Don't Produce, They Recruit." The entrepreneurial owner of the music store across the street wandered the sidewalks carrying a sign that simply said "Buy a Guitar." By the time the county commissioners got together to rescind the motion, claiming they had not realized what they were voting for when they passed it, the damage had been done. Dayton was again the laughingstock of the country, and rightly so. In the next local election, the community voted out of office all but one of the remaining county commissioners who took part in that vote. The rest had already resigned or chose not to run for reelection.

With the exception of June the Ten Commandments Lady, most of us were pretty angry at that county commission. Several Bryan College professors made it clear they didn't support the resolution, and local pastors confronted the out-of-town street preachers, begging them to leave. One church youth group handed out water at the gay pride rally as if to apologize on behalf of the community. Of course, such efforts received little coverage from the press, but I don't think it was because the reporters were out to "get us" again. I think they were just fascinated to discover in our hometown a small remnant of the kind of extreme religious separatism thought to be extinct in this country.

That's what's funny about this little town. When it comes to different breeds of Christianity, Dayton is a Galapagos Island of sorts, a terrific destination for anyone wishing to study the evolution of fundamentalism in America. We've got folks like June the Ten Commandments Lady shopping for groceries at the same produce stand as biblical scholars and apologists. On a given Sunday morning, one pastor will charge his congregation to love their enemies, another to consider the historical context of the book of Romans, and another to handle live rattlesnakes as an expression of faith. While some local parishioners insist on King-James-only services, a good many can read the text in the original Hebrew and Greek. While a few congratulated the county commission for their stand against homosexuality, most accused them of making Dayton look backward and out of touch.

The evangelical community has a curious reputation for resisting cultural movements before suddenly deciding to embrace them, and believers in Dayton are no different. These days most Christians, even conservative Christians, acknowledge that the Monkey Town approach of stubborn isolationism and anti-intellectualism is an outdated and ineffective strategy for expanding the kingdom.

It's hard to say for certain how the Scopes trial affected the Christian community in Dayton and around the world, but I have a feeling that after the cross-examination of William Jennings Bryan, a lot of evangelicals decided that something had to change. They decided that what happened on the witness stand that hot summer's day should never happen again. To survive in a modern world, they needed to be more prepared to respond to its questions. They could no longer simply resist evolutionary theory, secular humanism, higher criticism, and other modernist threats; they had to learn to effectively engage them instead. So after years of opposing any concept of survival of the fittest, a funny thing happened to the evangelical community in Dayton and around the country: it evolved.

CHAPTER 4

Greg the Apologist

My friend Greg grew up without rock-and-roll.
"Movies and dancing were out too," he explained, "as was theology."

Raised in a strict, King-James-only church that closely followed the teachings of evangelist Jerry Falwell, Greg describes his initial experience with Christianity as one that was "moralistic, reactionary, anti-intellectual, and atheological."

"It was like drowning in a pool of shallow water," he said.

So Greg rebelled — not with drugs, sex, or alcohol but with books.

He attended a Christian liberal arts college that, in the early nineties, emphasized engaging culture rather than resisting it. Intense and remarkably intelligent, Greg immediately caught on. He captured the attention of several faculty members, who saw in him the makings of a persuasive and charismatic apologist. He pored over stacks of theology books, asked precocious questions, wrote some impressive papers, and said he came to realize that "thinking was a Christian thing to do." A couple of degrees later, he was traveling across the country and the world, speaking on everything from bioethics to postmodernism to pluralism.

You never forget the first time you hear Greg speak. People describe it as trying to drink from a fire hydrant. Greg has a way of challenging his listeners to think bigger thoughts about God and the world than they ever dreamed possible. He moves from idea to idea seamlessly, always introducing a new concept just seconds before you think you've wrapped your brain around the last one. He knows how to talk to teenagers without being condescending and to seniors without sounding high and mighty.

I first encountered Greg when I was in high school and he spoke to my youth group about the all-encompassing nature of God's truth, how there is a biblical way to think about every- thing — from science, to philosophy, to pop culture, to technol- ogy. If we prepared ourselves to make a defense on behalf of the gospel, he said, there was no subject or discipline beyond the reach of the Light, no new idea or discovery we needed to fear. With the advantage of access to absolute truth, we had all that we needed to go out and change the world.

I remember that when I came home from youth group that night, my mother asked me what Greg talked about. "I don't remember exactly," I said, still struggling to absorb it. "But I think he was right."

Never quite forgetting that first impression, I decided to spend the summer after my junior year of college working with Greg at an intense, two-week apologetics seminar designed to introduce high school students to the concept of a biblical worldview. By that point, I'd become pretty proficient at making a defense for the gospel myself, so I served as a counselor, charged with guiding a small group of seventeen-year-old girls through the heady material.

I felt anxious to impress Greg and the other leaders at the conference, as well as the eight girls under my tutelage. I felt particularly burdened because some of my girls planned on attending state universities, where, I'd been told, they had a 70 percent chance of losing both their belief in absolute truth and their virginity. My job was to help prepare them to enter a secular, relativistic society knowing what they believed and why they believed it.

During the first few days of the conference, a range of speakers lectured on Darwinism, naturalism, transcendentalism, secularism, pluralism, and host of other isms that I felt comfortable enough discussing with my group. But by the end of the first week, after one speaker had condemned public schools as a lost cause, another denounced global warming as a radical leftist conspiracy, another decried modern art as nothing better than the scribbles of a five-year-old, and another attacked feminism as a threat to the biblical role of women in society, I began to worry that as a public high school graduate with an affinity for baby seals, Jackson Pollock, and pantsuits, I didn't have a Christian-enough worldview. I grew increasingly uncomfortable with how verses were lifted from the Bible to support political positions like gun rights, strong national defense, capital punishment, and limited intervention in the free market. These seemed more like Republican values than biblical values to me. I waited for Greg to object, but he never did.

It was the first time I wondered if perhaps there is no such thing as one, single biblical worldview, if perhaps there are as many worldviews out there as there are people.

At the conclusion of the seminar, Greg issued a stirring call for action, a charge for students to continue to study and learn, to fearlessly go out and change the world, and to always be ready with an answer in defense of their faith. He was passionate, clear, well studied, and prepared, the embodiment of how American fundamentalism adapted to modernism to become an aggressively intellectual, apologetics-driven counterculture. He was everything William Jennings Bryan failed to be on the witness stand in 1925.

The last time I interacted with Greg, we were engaged in a little email debate about how best to care for America's poor. These days it seems like he and I disagree on a lot of things: politics, theology, gender roles, environmentalism, economics, and so on. Sometimes I'm afraid that I've disappointed him. Sometimes I'm afraid that I'm wrong. But I hope Greg understands that in the same way he had to change to make sense of his faith, so I had to change to make sense of mine.

CHAPTER 5

When Skeptics Ask

By the time I graduated in 2003 from the college named in his honor, I'd resolved that what William Jennings Bryan should have said on the witness stand is this: Because the Bible is God's Word and is truthful in all that it affirms, the book of Genesis accurately records how God created the universe and life on earth. Based on the scientific accuracy of the Bible, one must conclude that the creation week consisted of seven twenty-four-hour days and that 1,656 years elapsed between the creation and the flood, 342 years elapsed between the flood and the birth of Abraham, and two thousand years elapsed between the birth of Abraham and the birth of Christ. Geological and fossil evidence does not conclusively prove an earth age of millions of years but can be explained by the argument that God chose to create things at full maturity with the appearance of having developed or by the argument that various factors, such as the earth's magnetic field, may have changed through the years and affected the accuracy of carbon dating. Contrary to the theory of evolution, the Bible teaches that God separately created distinct kinds of organisms and that the similarities between these organisms point to a common creator rather than a common origin. The theory of evolution fails to account for the degree of complexity inherent in biological organisms, to produce a sufficient fossil record of transitional species, and to explain the many ambiguities in biological classification. Therefore, it should not be taught as fact in public schools. Most important, the theory of evolution is dangerous because it undermines the authority of the Bible and threatens the foundation of Christianity.[4]

I learned most of this from Dr. Kurt Wise, one of the leading young-earth creationists in the country and a favorite professor among Bryan College students when I studied there. Armed with a degree in paleontology from Harvard University, Dr. Wise had studied under Stephen J. Gould, a renowned evolutionist and science writer. Dr. Wise said that his goal was to formulate a model of earth history consistent with both Scripture and the scientific data. An angular sort of person, with long legs and a wide gait, he moved about the campus at a deliberate and accelerated pace, as if he was always on his way to do something important. He enjoyed spending time with students in long conversations after class and in hiking and spelunking trips through the mountains.

Dr. Wise told us the story of how, as a sophomore in high school, he had dreams of becoming a scientist but could not reconcile the theory of evolution with the creation account found in the Bible. So one night, after the rest of his family had gone to bed, he took a pair of scissors and a newly purchased Bible and began cutting out every verse that he thought would have to be removed to believe in evolution. He spent weeks and weeks on the project, until he'd gone through the entire book, from Genesis to Revelation. By the time he finished, he said that he couldn't even lift the Bible without its falling apart. That was when he decided, "Either Scripture was true and evolution was wrong or evolution was true and I must toss out the Bible."[5]

In many ways, Dr. Wise embodied the spirit of Bryan College. While not everyone on campus supported young-earth creationism, the overriding principle behind the school's educational approach was that the Bible serves as our most reliable textbook, that it provides an infallible foundation on which to build the academic disciplines. We learned that everything from science to history, economics, art, psychology, politics, and literature can be studied from a "biblical worldview." The goal of a Bryan College education was to develop a comprehensive approach to life in which we looked at the world wearing Christian glasses.

I've never in my life encountered an organization so consistently on-message. I'm willing to bet that if I were to show up on campus today and ask a random student about his or her purpose for studying there, the response would be, "To develop a biblical worldview." We used to tell freshmen that if a professor called on them in class and caught them unprepared, the best strategy was to simply blurt out, "Worldview?" and hope for the best.

I came to Bryan College in 1999 both hungry for answers about Christianity and eager to prove my mastery of it. Having lived in Dayton for five years, I already knew most of my professors and was familiar with the Bryan campus and its traditions.

I knew, for instance, that instead of hazing freshmen, the senior class welcomed them by washing their feet. I knew that after the first snowfall, students used trays from the cafeteria as sleds. I knew that the three major worldviews are naturalism, transcendentalism, and theism, and that biblical Christianity falls into the theism category. I knew that the Bradford pears dotting the hilly, pastoral campus turn ruby red in the fall but smell funny when they bloom in the spring. I knew which dorms boasted the best views of the mountains, which professors most inspired their students, and which upperclassmen were considered cool.

My best friend, Sarah, and I had decided ahead of time to live in the same dorm but to room with girls we didn't already know so as not to get too cliquish. We lucked out on roommates and quickly developed new, long-lasting friendships. I immediately ran for student government and won my race for freshman representative to the senate, thanks mostly to my controversial campaign slogan: "Want Your Voice Heard? Go to Held." I majored in English but loaded my schedule with theology and Bible classes. It took some effort to hide my disappointment when a show of hands revealed that I wasn't the only one in my Introduction to the Bible class who was familiar with dispensationalism.

In keeping with the college's vision, I immediately took a required introductory course titled Biblical Worldview. In this class, I learned not only how to define and defend a biblical worldview but also how to dismantle opposing worldviews. My professor, a warm and affable theologian with a penchant for sweater vests, taught me that when defending my faith against atheists and agnostics, the best strategy was to ask questions, questions to which I already knew the answers, of course.

For example, if someone said to me, "You should be tolerant of other religions and belief systems," I should respond by asking, "What about the belief systems of Adolph Hitler and Joseph Stalin? Should I be tolerant of those?" Or if someone said, "I cannot believe in God because of all the injustice in the world," I should say, "Are you saying, then, that there is an absolute standard of right and wrong? Where do you get this standard? On what is it based?" If someone announced that the universe began with the big bang, I should ask, "Do you have any proof of that? If the world came into being by chance, how do you explain its intricate design?" If someone said, "There are no absolutes," I should ask, "Are you absolutely sure?"

In Biblical Worldview, we picked apart dozens of belief systems, from secular humanism to Buddhism. We examined their strengths and weaknesses and occasionally chuckled at their absurdities. Sometimes, for class projects or chapel programs, we performed skits. We learned to adopt the high-pitched tone and dazed expression of the stereotypical tree-hugging New Ager in order to explain that transcendentalists believed that "we are aaall god ... aaall one ... aaall okay," often concluding with a mock yoga pose and an exaggerated "ohm." (To be fair, we also made fun of ourselves in the skits, dressing up in cheesy Christian T-shirts and talking about how we'd burned all our secular CDs and kissed dating goodbye.)

The only worldview system that provides adequate answers to life's ultimate questions, my professor said, is biblical Christianity.

Looking through the glasses of a biblical worldview brought everything into focus; it made everything make sense. "All truth is God's truth," he said, "so as Christians, we can expect to see reality continually support our premise."

With this assurance, we studied common challenges to Christianity, such as the problem of evil and the destiny of the unevangelized. These were treated as issues that atheists and agnostics might raise to try to undermine Christianity, not issues that believers generally struggled with themselves, so I had to be careful how I phrased my questions in class.

One day I asked, "So, Dr. Jordan, what if ... what if my opponent challenges me by saying that if Christianity is the only path to salvation, that means the majority of the human population will be damned to hell?"

Dr. Jordan said something about how we all deserve hell anyway, something about falling short of the glory of God.

"Yes, but doesn't that mean that ... wouldn't my opponent charge that most people were just born at the wrong place and the wrong time, that they never even had the chance to be saved in the first place?"

Dr. Jordan said something about the importance of going into all the world to preach the gospel.

"Yes, but ... but what should I tell my opponent if she still thinks that's not fair?"

Dr. Jordan talked for a while about God's higher ways and then suggested that I use the opening to challenge my opponent about where she gets her standard for right and wrong, to suggest that with such a piqued conscience, she must believe in a universal standard of justice after all.

Before I had the time to say, "Yes, but won't she know I'm just changing the subject?" the guy sitting in the desk behind me whispered, "Rachel, wrap it up. Your opponent's about to argue right through my next class."

What was happening at Bryan College was happening in evangelical schools and churches across the country during the apologetics movement of the 1970s, '80s, and '90s. Born of the necessity to more effectively engage modernism and avoid embarrassments like the Scopes trial, the apologetics movement in America represented a significant evolution within the evangelical subculture, an evolution away from blind faith, anti-intellectualism, and cultural withdrawal toward hard rationalism, systematic theology, and political action. You might say it was the culmination of modern Enlightenment values applied specifically to religious dialogue.

Theologians like Francis Schaeffer, Norm Geisler, and Lee Strobel entered the scene, introducing words like *presupposition* and *worldview* to the common Christian's lexicon. These scholars claimed that if Christians would simply prepare themselves to reason with skeptics, armed with the right scientific, historical, and philosophical facts, they could convince even the most hardened atheist of the inherent truth of the biblical worldview. The hard evidence, they urged, supports Christianity. As Josh McDowell announced in his landmark book, *Evidence That*

Demands a Verdict, "I took the evidence that I could gather and put it on the scales. The scales tipped the way of Christ being the Son of God and resurrected from the dead." The validity of the Christian faith, he said, was "confirmed through investigation."[6]

With that in mind, the apostle Peter's command to "always be prepared to give an answer to everyone who asks" became a rallying cry for true believers during the apologetics movement. To be caught unready, like William Jennings Bryan on the witness stand, equaled outright disobedience to God and characterized what Francis Shaeffer called the "great evangelical disaster" of thoughtless faith. To fight the good fight, the most important weapon was the sword of absolute truth, and the goal of the Christian life was to learn how to use it. As Dr. David Noebel wrote in his mammoth volume *Understanding the Times,* "The battle lines have been drawn. As Christians armed with the truth — indeed, armed with the revelation of Truth Himself … we are more than equipped to shatter the myths of all opposing worldviews…. Truth is our greatest weapon."[7]

War imagery pervaded the aggressively intellectual apologetics movement. Dr. Noebel authored titles ranging from *The Homosexual Revolution* to *Mind Siege* to *The Battle for Truth.* Geisler, who earned himself the nickname "Stormin' Norman," began calmly enough with *Christian Apologetics* (1976) but grew increasingly militaristic with titles such as *Christianity Under Attack* (1985), *The Battle for the Resurrection* (1989), and *Battle for God* (2001). Drawing battle lines worked because, as the new millennium approached, evangelicals in America were indeed feeling threatened. In the years following the Scopes Monkey

Trial, the Supreme Court barred religious instruction from public schools and outlawed school-sponsored prayer. During the Cold War, fears that the United States was falling behind the Soviet Union in science and technology led Congress to support updating science textbooks to include evolutionary theory. Feminism threatened the church's patriarchal leadership system. Higher criticism challenged the accuracy of the Bible. The *Roe v. Wade* decision in 1973 left many Christians with the sense that their government had abandoned them. From keeping nativity scenes in public buildings to keeping "one nation under God" in the Pledge of Allegiance, defending America from the perceived takeover of secular humanism became the purpose of the modern church.

Never before had the words *Christian* and *biblical* been used so frequently as adjectives. Evangelicals read Christian books and listened to Christian music. They sent their kids to Christian colleges, where they received Christian educations. Apologists and theologians talked about the biblical approach to homosexuality, the biblical response to global warming, and the biblical view of parenting. The Moral Majority, and later the Christian Coalition, mobilized millions to political action, while James Dobson, founder of Focus on the Family, instructed his radio listeners to vote based on their Christian values. The election of George W. Bush in 2000 and his reelection in 2004 were widely attributed to the action of conservative evangelicals across the country who had been convinced that, as a born-again pro-lifer, Bush would take their side on the important moral issues. It was as though the Christian community sat perpetually on the witness stand, always ready for a fight, always ready to defend itself against the world, always ready to give an answer.

It was within this social context that I and an entire generation of young evangelicals constructed our Christian worldviews. You might say that we were born ready with answers. We grew up with a fervent devotion to the inerrancy of the Bible and learned that whatever the question might be, an answer could be found within its pages. We knew what atheists and humanists and Buddhists believed before we actually met any atheists or humanists or Buddhists, and we knew how to effectively discredit their worldviews before ever encountering them on our own. To experience the knowledge of Jesus Christ, we didn't need to be born again; we simply needed to be born. Our parents, our teachers, and our favorite theologians took it from there, providing us with all the answers before we ever had time to really wrestle with the questions.

My experience at Bryan was everything a college experience should be. I made lifelong friends, learned how to think critically, and became well versed in Christian apologetics. I maintained a solid-enough grade point average to participate in an array of extracurricular activities that taught me a lot about myself and how to work with other people. My love for literature grew more pronounced with each of Tennyson's alliterated lines and every frighteningly precise Flannery O'Connor character. Some of my English professors thought my writing showed potential. Best of all, I met and fell in love with a tall, handsome New Jersey boy, whom I married six months after earning my degree, thus fulfilling my mother's charge to go to a Christian college and marry a Christian boy. My classmates elected me their senior class president and asked me to deliver the commencement address on graduation day.

On the outside, I embodied all the expectations I had for myself going into college. I was confident, articulate, ready to change the world. But on the inside, something different was happening. I started to have doubts.

You might say that the apologetics movement had created a monster. I'd gotten so good at critiquing all the fallacies of opposing worldviews, at searching for truth through objective analysis, that it was only a matter of time before I turned the same skeptical eye upon my own faith. It occurred to me that in worldview class, we laughed at how transcendentalists so serenely embraced paradox and contradiction, but then went on to theology class and accepted without question that Jesus existed as both fully God and fully man. We criticized radical Islam as a natural outworking of the violent tone of the Qur'an without acknowledging the fact that the God of Israel ordered his people to kill every living thing in Canaan, from the elderly to the newborn. We sneered at the notion of climate change yet believed that God once made the earth stand still. We accused scientists of having an agenda, of ignoring science that contradicted the evolution paradigm, but engaged in some mental gymnastics of our own, trying to explain how it's possible to see the light from distant stars. We mocked New Age ambiguity but could not explain the nature of the Trinity. We claimed that ours was a rational, logical faith, when it centered on the God of the universe wrapping himself in flesh to be born in a manger in Bethlehem.

Most worrisome, however, was how we criticized relativists for picking and choosing truth, while our own biblical approach required some selectivity of its own. For example, I was taught that the Bible served as a guidebook for Christian dating and marriage, but no one ever suggested that my father had the right to sell me to the highest bidder or to take multiple wives, like Abraham. Homosexuality was preached against incessantly, but little was said of gluttony or greed. We decried the death of each aborted baby as a violation of the sanctity of human life but shrugged off the deaths of Iraqi children as expected collateral damage in a war against evil. We celebrated archeological finds that supported the historical claims of the Bible yet discounted massive amounts of scientific evidence in support of an old earth.

Despite my emerging doubts, I went on looking for ways to glue the pieces of my faith back together, trying to convince myself and my friends that everything was okay. In my commencement address, I assured the senior class that we were exceptionally prepared to answer life's questions, that our biblical worldview glasses would bring everything into focus, sharpening the contrast between black and white, right and wrong, evil and good. I said it, wanting desperately to believe it was true. I said it, knowing good and well that it wasn't going to be that simple. I said it, knowing that the world just didn't make that kind of sense anymore.

PART 2

CHALLENGE

CHAPTER 6

Nathan the Soldier

"Thanks for the coffee."

Nathan absently spun the cardboard sleeve around his macchiato as he scanned the nearly empty coffee shop where we'd met downtown. His eyes looked tired.

"Oh, it's the least I could do," I said. "Thanks for serving our country."

He grinned at me, and I remembered how his smile always carried a hint of irony, as if toying with a smirk. "You're welcome," he said, amusement in his voice. "Anytime."

Although Nathan and I had attended the same church for six years, we never had much in common until recently. A brown-eyed musician with a smoking habit and ridiculously high IQ, he'd always been a bit of a skeptic. His questions in youth group used to make me uncomfortable. Now, nearly a decade after we graduated from high school together, they made perfect sense.

At the coffee shop that afternoon, Nathan told me about Fort Hood and Iraq, about Middle Eastern culture and learning Arabic, about the roadside bomb that hit his vehicle, about how he hadn't been able to relax or let down his guard or sleep peacefully since then, about his frustrations with organized religion, about how he still wanted to help the homeless and hungry, about how he desperately missed his piano.

"I guess after you spend so much time in another country," he said, "you start to realize how similar everyone really is, how there's not that much difference between us. These people break my heart, Rachel—even the ones I'm supposed to consider my enemies, even the guy who pushed a button somewhere and blew up my vehicle, even the guy who leaves bombs under bridges or blows himself up at checkpoints. I'm not saying they're right or they aren't responsible for their actions, but most of them are just doing what they sincerely believe to be God's will. Most are just as lost and screwed up as the rest of us."

A small group of Bryan students was engaged in a Bible study at a table in the corner.

Nathan leaned in, lowering his voice. "I'm not trying to offend you or anybody, but there's this attitude that we're Americans, we're right, and God is on our side, and they're Muslims, so they're wrong, and God wants us to defeat them. People think we're over there fighting a one-dimensional enemy. They think we're over there fighting evil."

He looked at me as if waiting for an objection.

"That's what they tell us at the press conferences," I said.

His smile succumbed to the smirk, and we both laughed a little.

"Take one of my old chaplains, for example," Nathan said. "He insisted on coming to every mission briefing right before we loaded up vehicles and rolled out the gates, and he always delivered this bombastic prayer about God protecting us and giving us victory over our enemies and so forth and so on. Now, I'm not saying whether there is divine intervention when it comes to our safety and health or whatever, but I just kept thinking about all the Iraqi mothers praying at that very moment for God to protect their sons who were engaged in direct conflict with us. So my chaplain is absolutely convinced that God is on our side, while they are absolutely convinced that God is on their side. And I started to wonder, really, what's the difference between us?"

"I know what you mean," I said. "Well, I guess I don't know exactly what you mean — I've not been to Iraq or anything — but I get what you're saying. It's like, as soon as you're able to step into someone else's shoes or look at the world from a different perspective, everything you believe becomes less certain, or at least less black and white."

"I've gotten to know some Muslims pretty well," Nathan said. "And that's really changed my perspective. They're not all violent fundamentalists. They don't all hate America. In fact, the Muslim guy that helped me learn Arabic is a heck of a lot more devoted to his faith than most Christians I know. He fasted all through Ramadan, loves his family, is an honest, upstanding guy. I learned a lot from him. It's just hard for me to judge him, you know? It's hard for me to say, 'Hey, you're going to hell because you didn't grow up in a Christian home like me.'"

"That's something I've been struggling with myself," I said. "If evangelical Christians are the only ones going to heaven, then that leaves a whole lot of people in hell. It leaves most people in hell, actually. I'm not sure I can believe that's true."

Nathan studied his coffee for a moment and a heavy silence fell between us. I thought about how much this silence would have frightened me a few years ago, back when I thought I always had to be ready with an answer.

"It's hard sometimes because most people just freak out whenever I talk about this stuff," Nathan said. "Sometimes I think they are afraid that I've backslidden, that I'm going to get killed in Iraq and go to hell or something."

He shifted uncomfortably in his chair before continuing. "It's not like I haven't grappled with my own mortality. I'm a realist. It's just that people keep saying things like 'This is not your home' and 'We were made for heaven.' I know they're just trying to make me feel better about how messed up things are, but it makes me want to say, 'Well, then why don't I just go blow my brains out and get it over with?' I don't really mean it, of course. It's just that people talk as if nothing we do this side of eternity matters. It's all pointless. We're just waiting to die. And I wonder, then why don't we just get it over with?"

"Maybe salvation isn't just about eternity," I said. "Maybe God wants to save us from something in the present, something in the here and now."

"Like what?"

"Like — I don't know — maybe our sins, maybe our circumstances, maybe even our religion."

"That's an interesting way to look at it," Nathan said.

"Yeah, I'm still trying to figure it out."

"You know what I like best about Jesus?" Nathan asked. "How he really took care of poor people. That's one of the few things about the Christian faith that still makes sense to me after all of this. I know it sounds crazy, but whenever I'm back in Texas, I go to this knitting group every month to help make blankets for homeless people. I'm like the only guy in the group and I'm definitely the youngest."

I couldn't help but laugh. Nathan didn't seem like the knitting type.

"It's a little thing that probably doesn't make that big of an impact in the grand scheme of things. Honestly, for the amount of money I spend on beer in a given weekend, I could probably just go out and buy a bunch of brand-new blankets for every homeless guy in town. But something about sitting in a circle with those ladies doing something for somebody else makes me feel closer to God. It's like my church."

We talked for a few more hours in the coffee shop that day, followed by a regular correspondence over email. Nathan went back to Texas and then back to Iraq for a second tour of duty. Sometimes I wished I could mail him a piano.

CHAPTER 7

When Believers Ask

It didn't feel like a faith crisis right away—more like a faith malfunction, a little glitch in the system that made a few critical functions start to misfire. It began one November afternoon as I hurried through the lobby of my dorm at Bryan on my way to a meeting with the newspaper staff. I noticed a group of ten or twelve girls standing around the TV.

"Did something happen?" I asked, my stomach dropping, as I remembered a similar scene from the morning of September 11.

"You've got to see this," one of the girls said.

It was just before the US invaded Afghanistan in 2001, and the press had been airing a series of crude home videos depicting the human rights abuses of the Taliban. The most recent footage came from *Behind the Veil*, an undercover documentary that highlights the oppression of women in that country.

My classmates and I watched as a woman enshrouded in a heavy blue burqa arrived at a soccer stadium in Kabul in the back of a pickup truck. Accused of murdering her husband, she was flanked by Kalishnikov-toting Taliban officers who, according to the narrator, intended to make an example of her before the nearly thirty thousand spectators. The documentary suddenly jumped to the next clip, in which the woman was forced to kneel on the dusty soccer pitch. She turned to the left and right, as if disoriented. The camera's zoom was so tight that everything trembled.

Then, from the left-hand corner of the screen, an executioner approached the woman, methodically lifted his gun to the back of her head, and fired. Several of the girls in the lobby gasped. The documentary suddenly cut to the next image, in which another veiled woman rushed to the body to make sure it was still properly hidden by the burqa. The woman's lifeless form lay face up, and I noticed that she wore tennis shoes.

I later learned that her name was Zarmina. She was a thirty-five-year-old mother of five whose husband had a reputation for abuse. She had married him when she was just sixteen. The Taliban never found a murder weapon, but locals report that they got a confession after beating Zarmina for two days with steel cables. Convicted in a secret trial, Zarmina spent three years in an Afghan prison, while her oldest daughters were sold into sex slavery by relatives. Friends say she came to the soccer stadium expecting a series of lashes, not death.

CNN repeatedly aired the tape, perhaps to make us feel better about going to war against the Taliban. But it wasn't the Taliban I was angry with. Each time I watched Zarmina's execution, I got angrier and angrier with God. God was the one who claimed to have formed Zarmina in her mother's womb. It was God who ordained that she be born in a third-world country under an oppressive regime. God had all the power and resources at his disposal to stop this from happening, and yet he did nothing. Worst of all, twenty years of Christian education assured me that because Zarmina was a Muslim, she would suffer unending torment in hell for the rest of eternity. How the Taliban punished Zarmina in this life was nothing compared with how God would punish her in the next.

Suddenly abstract concepts about heaven and hell, election and free will, religious pluralism and exclusivism had a name: Zarmina. I felt like I could come to terms with Zarmina's suffering if it were restricted to this lifetime, if I knew that God would grant her some sort of justice after death. But the idea that this woman passed from agony to agony, from torture to torture, from a lifetime of pain and sadness to an eternity of pain and sadness, all because she had less information about the gospel than I did, seemed cruel, even sadistic. God knew long before Zarmina was born — before her first giggle, before her first steps, before her first words — that this was her fate. He knew it from the beginning and yet created her anyway. I wondered how many millions of people like Zarmina died every day in similar circumstances. I thought about the Killing Fields of Cambodia, the gassing of Iraqi Kurds, and those terrible, haunting images of warehouses full of eyeglasses and shoes and prayer shawls left behind by victims of the Holocaust. Was I supposed to believe that all of these people went to hell because they weren't Christians?

It wasn't as if the concept of hell had never bothered me before. Even as a child, I had a strange habit of thinking about people in terms of their eternal destiny. Whenever I caught a news story about the death of a movie star or politician, I asked my parents if he or she was a Christian. When I learned about Pizarro's slaughter of the Incas in history class, I asked my teacher if there was any chance that more benevolent missionaries might have reached the natives first. I cried through the end of *Life Is Beautiful* because I believed that if Guido had been a real person, he would have gone to hell.

After we finished the last pages of *The Diary of Anne Frank* in middle school, Mrs. Kelly informed the class that Anne and her sister died of typhus in a prison camp, thanks to Adolf Hitler. I was horrified, not just because of the prison camp but because everything I'd been taught as a girl told me that because Anne was Jewish, because she had not accepted Jesus Christ as her Savior, she and the rest of her family were burning in hell. I remember staring at the black-and-white picture of Anne on the cover of my paperback, privately begging God to let her out of the lake of fire. For weeks, I prayed diligently for her departed soul, even though I'd heard that only Catholics and Mormons ever did such a thing. I was a pretty intense kid, actually.

In Sunday school, they always make hell out to be a place for people like Hitler, not a place for his victims. But if my Sunday school teachers and college professors were right, then hell will be populated not only by people like Hitler and Stalin, Hussein and Milosevic but by the people that they persecuted. If only born-again Christians go to heaven, then the piles of suitcases and bags of human hair displayed at the Holocaust Museum represent thousands upon thousands of men, women, and children suffering eternal agony at the hands of an angry God. If salvation is available only to Christians, then the gospel isn't good news at all. For most of the human race, it is terrible news.

I thought about all of this the night after I saw Zarmina's execution. A heavy rain clawed at my dorm room window like a frantic cat, and the wind rattled the power lines so that the lamplight flickered on and off. Sarah sat in the opposite corner of the room on the floor, working feverishly on some kind of poster project for her elementary education class, scraps of construction paper and little plastic eyeballs spread all around her. I couldn't concentrate on my *King Lear* assignment.

"Do you think that there is rape in hell?" I asked Sarah.

"What?" She looked understandably startled.

"Rape. Do you think there is rape in hell?"

"I don't know, Rachel. I don't think the Bible says anything about that. What on earth makes you ask?"

"People say that hell is a place of eternal torture, right? Well, the most horrible thing I can imagine happening to anybody is getting raped over and over again for eternity, so I suppose it's fathomable that people get raped in hell, right?"

"I guess it's fathomable, but — "

"Did you see that thing on the news about that woman who got shot at the soccer field in Afghanistan?"

"Yeah, I did."

"What do you think happened to her after that?"

"After she got shot? I don't think we can know for sure, Rachel. We don't really know her heart."

"That's what people say when they don't want to say that someone went to hell," I said flatly. "The lady on CNN said she prayed the traditional Muslim prayers just before they brought her out. She was definitely a Muslim, Sarah."

Sarah paused. "Well, you know Jesus said, 'I am the way, the truth, and the life …'"

"But that's not fair. How was she supposed to know any different? All her life she was taught that Islam is the only true religion, just like we were taught all our lives that Christianity is the only true religion. God didn't really give her a chance."

"Isn't that why missionaries are so important?" Sarah asked.

"Yes, but missionaries can't get to everybody in time. There are millions of people, past and present, who have had no exposure to Christianity at all. Are we supposed to believe that five seconds after Jesus rose from the dead, everyone on earth was responsible for that information? How is a guy living in, I don't know, Outer Mongolia in 15 AD supposed to figure out that Jesus died on the cross for his sins, was buried, and rose again on the third day? It's impossible."

I had absolutely no idea where Outer Mongolia was or what sort of people lived there in 15 AD, but I was pretty certain they didn't go to Sunday school.

"We just assume that little kids and mentally disabled people go to heaven," I said. "The Bible doesn't come right out and say that. So why can't we believe that people without the gospel go to heaven? What's the difference? Why won't anyone give me a straight answer on this?"

Poor Sarah looked stricken, and I realized I may have pushed a little too hard.

"Why don't you ask your dad?" she asked tentatively.

That night I took a long shower before going to bed, where I lay awake for hours listening to the rain and trying to pray. When I finally fell asleep, I dreamed about Zarmina.

The next morning, chapel opened with worship. Onstage a guy wearing jeans, a gray T-shirt, and Birkenstocks played the guitar, the lyrics of the worship song projected on the screen behind him. We sang a song in which the lyrics said of God, "You're altogether lovely, altogether worthy, altogether wonderful to me."

As my friends and classmates sang together, some with raised hands and closed eyes, all I could think about was Zarmina's tennis shoes peeking out from under her burqa. I didn't see anything lovely or wonderful about that. My throat tightened, and I stopped singing. A thick and intense sadness rushed over my body, and I didn't want to worship anymore.

All my life, I had imagined God as a warm, faceless light, a sort of benevolent and eternal sunshine. That morning in chapel, a shadow passed over him like an eclipse, and for the next few years, all I could see was a faint glow around its edges.

It was as if I had discovered a giant crack in the biblical worldview wall, and the more I studied that crack, the more fractures and fissures I noticed growing out of it. I began to worry that this thing with Zarmina might be a foundational problem, that there might be something seriously wrong with Christianity, something that can't be fixed.

What makes a faith crisis so scary is that once you allow

yourself to ask one or two questions, more inevitably follow. Before you know it, everything looks suspicious. Doubts I'd been shoving to the back of my mind for years came rushing forward in an avalanche of questions: If God is really good and merciful, then why did he command Joshua to kill every man, woman, and child in Jericho? Wouldn't we call that genocide today? How can God be fair and just if he preordains our eternal destiny, if most people have no choice but to face eternal damnation? When we say that God is sovereign, that no good or evil is done outside of his will, does that mean that he presides over every rape of a child? If we are born depraved and we have no control over our sin nature, why does God punish us for it? If all truth is God's truth, then why are we so afraid to confront the mountain of scientific evidence in support of evolution? Isn't it a little suspicious that the only true religion is the one with which we happened to grow up?

The space between doubting God's goodness and doubting his existence is not as wide as you might think. I found myself crossing it often, as it didn't require much of a leap. I suppose it's similar to what happens to a person when she is betrayed by a loved one. At first, the betrayed is angry because the betrayer has violated some sacred bond between them, some official or unofficial commitment to love, friendship, or loyalty. But over time, the betrayed begins to wonder if that bond ever existed in the first place, if it was real or just in her imagination. That's how I felt about God. First I doubted that he is good; then I doubted that he is real. It seemed the teleological argument in support of his existence was a lot less effective when I was unsure of his benevolence. I never realized how important hope is to belief.

I began collecting evidence for the little trial I was conducting in my head. I looked into the science behind evolution. I checked out books from the school library about world religions. I confronted the unflattering parts of church history. I studied troubling biblical texts that seemed to support slavery, misogyny, violence, and ethnic cleansing. I grew more and more suspicious of people who claimed that God supported certain political positions or theological systems or lifestyle decisions.

Big questions have a sort of domino effect. Concerns about certain biblical texts led to questions about the Bible's accuracy; questions about the Bible's accuracy led to questions about how the canon was assembled; questions about how the canon was assembled led to questions about church authority; questions about church authority led to questions about the Holy Spirit; questions about the Holy Spirit led to questions about the Trinity; questions about the Trinity led to questions about how on earth I'd gone from worrying about the garden of Eden to worrying about three-leaf clover analogies.

Only this time, I wasn't asking these questions rhetorically or in preparation for an imaginary debate with a skeptic. I was asking them because I didn't know. This time, I was the skeptic.

When I was a little girl, if someone asked me why I was a Christian, I said it was because Jesus lived in my heart. In high school, I said it was because I accepted the atonement of Jesus Christ on the cross for my sins. My sophomore year of college, during a short-lived Reformed phase, I said it was because of the irresistible grace of God. But after watching Zarmina's execution on television, I decided that the most truthful answer to that question was this: I was a Christian because I was born in the United States of America in the year 1981 to Peter and Robin Held. Arminians call it free will; Calvinists call it predestination. I call it "the cosmic lottery."

It doesn't take an expert in anthropology to figure out that the most important factor in determining the nature of one's existence, including one's religion, is the place and time in which one is born, a factor completely out of one's control. I happened to be born in the United States of America in the twentieth century to Christian parents whose religion I embraced. Had I lived in this very spot in the Appalachian mountains just two thousand years earlier, I know for a fact I would not have accepted Jesus Christ as my Lord and Savior, mainly because I would have never heard of the guy. Or let's say I got the century right but the location wrong. There's little doubt in my mind that if I had grown up in a modern Muslim household in, say, Afghanistan or Turkey, I would have faithfully honored the teachings of my parents and followed Islam like everyone else. We don't choose our worldviews; they are chosen for us.

That's what I told my father in his office one Friday afternoon, sometime between seeing Zarmina's execution and graduating from Bryan a year later.

I loved my father's office. Dense with books and heavy, dark furniture, it was decorated with miniature gargoyles and interesting rocks and framed photographs from my father's travels: a black bear among the wildflowers at Yellowstone, driftwood on a Bahamian beach, a perfect, sunlit shot of the Colosseum at Rome. An ornate wooden chess set waited on a corner table for impromptu games with students. Embarrassing pictures of me and Amanda in braces sat on his cluttered desk. I felt safe there.

"It's like God runs some kind of universal sweepstakes with humanity in which all of our names get thrown into a big hat at the beginning of time," I said, sitting cross-legged in the chair across from his desk. "Some of us are randomly selected for famine, war, disease, and paganism, while others end up with fifteen-thousand-square-foot houses, expensive Christian educations, and Double Stuf Oreos. It's a cosmic lottery, luck of the draw."

My father listened attentively, asking questions here and there and letting me go on for at least an hour before saying, "Rachel, we don't get to pick and choose which parts of the Bible we believe based on how we feel. Just because you don't understand God's ways doesn't mean he is not good. You're right. A lot of people die without the gospel, and I can see why that would upset you. But don't be ungrateful for your own salvation."

"Dad, how can I be grateful?" I asked incredulously, tears collecting in my eyes. "It's like God is a Nazi prison-camp guard, randomly weeding out prisoners as part of selection. If someone shot and killed Mom and Amanda but spared my life, maybe I'd feel a fleeting sense of gratitude toward him, but I could never bring myself to worship and adore him. How is God any different? Why should I worship a God who shows mercy to me but not my neighbor? Why should we be outraged by things like the Holocaust or human trafficking when our own God is just as cruel to his creation as we are to each other?"

I think my irreverence startled him a little, because something that looked like fear cast a shadow over his face. His voice sounded strained. "Rachel," he said gently, "be careful of what you say."

I think you officially grow up the moment you realize you are capable of causing your parents pain. All the rebellion of adolescence, all the slammed doors and temper tantrums and thoughtless words of youth — those are signs that you still think your parents are invincible, that you still imagine yourself as powerless against them. As my father and I talked in his office that afternoon, I imagined how devastated he would be if I ever left the faith, and I realized for the first time that I could break his heart. I realized for the first time that we were made out of the same stuff. Fear and insecurity felt the same to him as they felt to me. He had no special immunity against disappointment or guilt, no built-in armor to protect himself from the pain I might cause him. For the first time in my life, I knew what it was like to relate to my father as a peer.

It was scary.

CHAPTER 8

Jesus, God in Sandals

So this is the point in the story where I turn to Jesus.

Don't worry. There's no altar call or soft light or repetitious droning of "Just as I Am," no sudden realization that all of my questions are answered in a single verse, every doubt cast away by a moment of illumination, just me in my sweats with a glass of wine and the familiar stories of Jesus spread before me on the kitchen table like an old family photo album that suddenly carries new meaning after a death or a divorce or a long overdue reconciliation.

Three years had passed since I first saw Zarmina's execution on TV, and I was as angry with God as ever. Not because of any sadness in my own life — I was married, working for the local newspaper, and busy decorating our newly purchased home — but because of the deep, entrenched sadness of this world, a world in which thirty thousand children die of hunger every day, a world in which tsunami waves wash away entire villages, a world in which the gap between the rich and the poor continues to grow wider.

As a sort of last resort, I decided to commit the summer of

2004 to reading through the Gospels. I remembered something my youth pastor used to say in his sermons. "We're going to stop by the New Testament to see what Jesus has to say about this," he would announce before citing chapter and verse, "because Jesus embodied all of God's desires and passions and hopes and dreams, because Jesus was God in sandals."

I always loved that image: God in sandals. Nothing is quite so absurd or profound as the notion of the Great I AM walking around with dirt between his toes. I thought about this often as I wrestled with questions about God's nature and doubts about his goodness. I recalled what John said about Jesus in the opening lines of his gospel: "No one has seen God at any time; the only begotten God who is in the bosom of the Father, *He has explained Him*" (John 1:18 NASB, italics mine). I wanted an explanation from God, and according to John, the best place to start is with Jesus. If Jesus was really the most complete and comprehensive revelation of the divine, if he was indeed God in sandals, then that means he cared about what God cared about, hated what God hated, and loved what God loved. The incarnation gave God a face. It gave him literal tears, literal laughter, literal hands, literal feet, a literal heart, and a literal mind. What the Spirit of God said and did while living among us in the person of Jesus must say a lot about what matters most to him. So in spite of my doubts, or perhaps because of them, I decided to see if Jesus had the answer.

Well, he didn't. You can't get too far into the Gospels without noticing that Jesus made a pretty lousy apologist. I'm convinced he would have flunked out of any halfway decent Christian liberal arts institution. Jesus responded more with questions than with answers. He preferred story to exposition. Despite boasting infinite wisdom and limitless knowledge, Jesus chose not to overtly address religious pluralism, the problem of evil, hermeneutics, science, or homosexuality. He didn't provide bullet-point answers for detractors or lengthy explanations to doubters. He didn't make following him logical or easy. And yet I wasn't disappointed. Perhaps it was the wine. Perhaps it was the surprising relief of getting swept away in the story. But something about Jesus made me ask better questions. Something about Jesus gave me just enough hope to decide not to give up ... at least not yet.

The first thing I noticed while reading through Matthew, Mark, Luke, and John was that Christians who claim to take the Bible literally or who say they obey all of his teachings without "picking and choosing" are either liars or homeless. Jesus asked a lot of his disciples. "None of you can be My disciple who does not give up all his own possessions" (Luke 14:33 NASB). "Anyone who loves his father or mother more than me is not worthy of me" (Matt. 10:37). "If anyone would come after me, he must deny himself and take up his cross daily and follow me" (Luke 9:23).

Now, some argue that these instructions were meant specifically for those disciples charged with serving alongside Jesus during his ministry. This may be true, but even in the Sermon on the Mount, which was intended for a much broader audience, Jesus told the first Christians, "Do not resist an evil person. If someone strikes you on the right cheek, turn to him the other also. And if someone wants to sue you and take your tunic, let him have your cloak as well. If someone forces you to go one mile, go with him two miles. Give to the one who asks you, and do not turn away from the one who wants to borrow from you.... Love your enemies and pray for those who persecute you.... Do not store up for yourself treasures on earth.... Do not judge" (Matt. 5:39 – 42, 44; 6:19; 7:1). The teachings of Jesus fly in the face of all we are told by our culture and even by the church about setting boundaries, getting even, achieving financial success, and "calling sin a sin."

For the first time, I asked myself if my reservations about Christianity were purely ideological. I wondered if perhaps counting the cost played a subtle role. You'd have to be crazy not to have second thoughts about following Jesus.

The second theme that emerged while reading the Gospels is that, if Jesus is God, then God has not forgotten the downtrodden and oppressed of this world. In fact, Jesus had a special relationship with the most forgotten of first-century society: women, tax collectors, sick people, minorities, Samaritans, and sinners. Jesus welcomed children into his arms and washed his disciples' dirty feet. He took those suffering from leprosy by the hand and surrounded himself with the poor and uneducated. Jesus began his first sermon by explaining not that the poor are unlucky victims of the cosmic lottery but that theirs is the kingdom of heaven (Luke 6:20). Even when the crowds got so big that people were stepping all over each other, even when the beggars became loud and obnoxious, even when all the neediness and desperation embarrassed the disciples, time and time again Matthew describes Jesus as being "moved with compassion" (Matt. 9:36; 14:14; 15:32; 20:34 NKJV). Cautiously, I began to wonder if the reason I was so desperate to believe that God loved Zarmina was because he does.

The final and most startling thing I noticed as I grew more acquainted with the Gospels was that Jesus had a very different view of faith than the one to which I was accustomed. I'm not sure when it happened, but sometime in my late teens or early twenties, it was as if Jesus packed his bags and moved from my heart into my head. He became an idea, a sort of theological mechanism by which salvation was attained. I described him in terms of *atonement, logos, the object of my faith*, and *absolute truth*. He was something I agreed to, not someone I followed. Perhaps because I spent so much time as a student, I thought about faith in terms of believing the right things about Jesus. Born of a virgin? Check. Fully God and fully man? Check. Without sin? Check. Sacrificed on the cross on our behalf? Check. Checking the right things off the list meant the difference between salvation and damnation. It was what separated Christians from non-Christians, or as I liked to say, believers from nonbelievers.

But Jesus rarely framed discipleship in terms of intellectual assent to a set of propositional statements. He didn't walk new converts down the Romans Road or ask Peter to draft a doctrinal statement before giving him the keys to the kingdom. His method of evangelism varied from person to person and generally involved a dramatic change of lifestyle rather than a simple change of mind. To Jesus, "by faith alone" did not mean "by belief alone." To Jesus, faith was invariably linked to obedience.

Nowhere is this more evident than in the short parable he

told at the conclusion of his Sermon on the Mount: "Therefore everyone who hears these words of mine and puts them into practice is like a wise man who built his house on the rock. The rain came down, the streams rose, and the winds blew and beat against that house; yet it did not fall, because it had its foundation on the rock. But everyone who hears these words of mine and does not put them into practice is like a foolish man who built his house on sand. The rain came down, the streams rose, and the winds blew and beat against that house, and it fell with a great crash" (Matt. 7:24 – 27).

We used to sing a song about this in Sunday school that involved a lot of cool motions that showed exactly how the rains came down and the floods came up, how the wise man's house stood firm, and how the foolish man's house went *splat*! Through the years, I heard about how the story represents the importance of building my house on the solid rock of a biblical worldview, about how the best way to protect my faith against the winds and rain of doubt is to build it with the concrete of absolute truth, the joists of inerrant Scripture, and the bearing walls of sound Christian doctrine. And yet, in the words of Jesus, all those apologetics courses and theology books and debating techniques are just castles in the sand without a commitment to love my neighbor as myself. I began to wonder if obedience — with or without answers — was the only thing that could save me from this storm.

Needless to say, that was a strange summer. It wasn't the summer that brought an end to my doubt, but it was the summer I encountered a different Jesus, a Jesus who requires more from me than intellectual assent and emotional allegiance; a Jesus who associated with sinners and infuriated the religious; a Jesus who broke the rules and refused to cast the first stone; a Jesus who gravitated toward sick people and crazy people, homeless people and hopeless people; a Jesus who preferred story to exposition and metaphor to syllogism; a Jesus who answered questions with more questions, and demands for proof with demands for faith; a Jesus who taught his followers to give without expecting anything in return, to love their enemies to the point of death, to live simply and without a lot of stuff, and to say what they mean and mean what they say; a Jesus who healed each person differently and saved each person differently; a Jesus who had no list of beliefs to check off, no doctrinal statement to sign, no surefire way to tell who was "in" and who was "out"; a Jesus who loved after being betrayed, healed after being hurt, and forgave while being nailed to a tree; a Jesus who asked his disciples to do the same.

We all go to the Bible looking for something: sometimes it's comfort in the midst of sorrow; sometimes it's confirmation of what we already believe; sometimes it's facts to add wrinkles to our brains. I went to the Gospels looking for hope for Zarmina and answers to my questions about God. What I found was hope for Zarmina and about a million more questions about God. It occurred to me that if my faith managed to survive all of these doubts, then this radical rabbi, this God in sandals, would require more from me than ever before. This radical Jesus wanted to live not only in my heart and in my head but also in my hands, as I fed the hungry, reached out to my enemies, healed the sick, and comforted the lonely. Being a Christian, it seemed, isn't about agreeing to a certain way; it is about embodying a certain way. It is about living as an incarnation of Jesus, as Jesus lived as an incarnation of God. It is about being Jesus ... in tennis shoes.

CHAPTER 9

Survivor's Guilt

It's hard to maintain a consistent worldview when the world itself is always changing, and in the months and years following my junior year of college, the world changed dramatically.

Evangelicals helped elect George W. Bush to office in 2000 in hopes that he might win a few culture wars, but by the time he reached his second term, the country was embroiled in two actual wars that had changed the cultural landscape of the US and the world in ways never before imagined.

The religious nationalism that characterized the months after September 11, 2001, gave way to concern and doubt as a war-weary and economically struggling public grappled with the country's diminishing influence abroad. Pledges to "rid the world of evildoers," once unifying reveilles, rang with arrogance and naiveté in hindsight. Months turned into years, death tolls crept higher and higher, and talk of torture and wiretaps and collateral damage rose from nervous whispers to shouts. Things stopped fitting into the neat and tidy categories of right and wrong, good and evil. Black and white slowly bled into gray.

My friends and I watched it all unfold on our laptops and cell phones. Images of conflict and disaster arrived instantly and ran perpetually through the twenty-four-hour news cycle. No previous generation enjoyed such easy access to information or experienced such a profound sense of connectedness to the rest of the world. Because of this, I think we were less inclined than our parents to think of America as the center of the universe and the people of other countries and cultures as mere statistics. Shifts in immigration patterns meant we knew more Muslims and Hindus by name. The accessibility of international travel broadened our exposure to languages and cultures outside of the Western world. Our fondness for technology led us to read blogs from Ireland and tweets from Iran. We played poker with Australians and lost first-person shooter games to ten-year-old Korean kids. People like Zarmina seemed a lot less like "them" and a lot more like "us."

When Baghdad is virtually no farther away than New York, you begin to realize that what happens over there is just as real as what happens in your hometown. After seeing Zarmina's execution on TV, I began to grapple with the reality that kids who died in wars in the Middle East were no different from kids who died in terrorist attacks here in the US. Women raped in Darfur are no different from my mother or my sister or my roommate. Babies killed by bad water or lack of nutrition have no less value than babies killed in abortions. Afghan and Pakistani mothers don't love their children any less than American mothers love theirs.

I'm not sure if there was more bad news or if I was just paying more attention, but it seemed like the years following my graduation from Bryan in 2003 were turbulent ones for a lot of people around the world. Images of tsunami waves, earthquake rubble, and refugee camps filled newspapers and magazines. With each new report, I worked out the numbers in my head. The Asian tsunami of 2004, for example, killed two hundred thousand people living in coastal communities around Indonesia, Sri Lanka, India, and Thailand. That was nearly seventy times the death toll from the 9/11 attacks. Most of the victims were either Buddhist or Hindu. The conflict in Sudan that began in 2003 has claimed more than three hundred thousand men, women, and children, most of them Muslim. By the time the Kashmir earthquake of 2005 killed seventy thousand Pakistanis, just two months after Hurricane Katrina, the media claimed that the American public was suffering from what they called "disaster fatigue." I found this a little ironic, seeing as most Americans are well fed, perfectly safe, and wealthy by global standards.

While Iraqis were dodging car bombs and Pakistanis were pulling their children out of rubble, I was going to the movies with my friends, earning a decent living as a freelance writer, and splurging on name-brand cereal. While millions of people lived without access to the Bible, we had three different versions on our bookshelf. While Sudanese mothers worried about how to feed their children, we worried about beating the crowds to Olive Garden on Sunday. While some went a lifetime without hearing the gospel, we took it for granted.

"I'm not suffering from disaster fatigue," I told the television one day. "I'm suffering from survivor's guilt."

My generation tends to be suspicious of absolutism. Speakers at apologetics camp like to say that we're getting so open-minded our brains are falling out. A few go so far as to blame it all on Madonna and Lady Gaga. If they make it cool to be tolerant of other religions or give to charity or oppose war, they say, my generation will naively obey, buying Kabbalah bracelets, learning yoga, and joining the Free Tibet movement.

But I think most folks are beginning to realize that this assessment mischaracterizes my generation and underestimates how profoundly the world has changed for us. Nathan questioned religious exclusivism not because some celebrity told him to but because he spent time in Iraq, learned Arabic, and befriended a Muslim. I reexamined my positions on heaven and hell not because I wanted to be like Britney but because I was forever changed after watching Zarmina's execution. My friend Wendee, a biology student, opened her mind to the science behind evolutionary theory not because she was intellectually lazy but because she was curious and smart and committed to her field. My sister, Amanda, got behind AIDS-awareness campaigns not because she's a Bono fan but because she held a dying Indian girl in her arms.

My dad likes to explain it this way: "When I was growing up, my parents told me to finish my dinner because kids in Africa were dying of hunger. Now my children know those kids by name."

The open-mindedness of young adults reflects something more profound and important than a fad. I'm not exactly sure what it is yet or what it should be called, but I think it has something to do with adapting to a new environment, evolving in order to survive. After all, we grew up believing that the US was invincible, free-market capitalism was infallible, and Pluto was a planet. We've gotten used to changing our minds.

Some Christians are more offended by the idea of everyone going to heaven than by the idea of everyone going to hell. I learned this the hard way, as reports about my faith crisis spread around town and rumors that I'd become a universalist found their way back to me in a wave of concerned emails and phone calls. Once news of your backsliding makes it to the prayer chain, it's best just to resign yourself to your fate. I knew that my chances for winning another Best Christian Attitude Award were all but extinct when a former professor asked me when I'd started studying Buddhism.

Privately, I felt frightened and lost. I cried out to God night after night, begging him to "help me in my unbelief." I pressed my face into my pillow, trying to will myself out of doubt and back to faith, only to wake up the next morning with puffy red eyes and a spiritual numbness that left me absent and disconnected from the world. I hated going to church because silly little things like communion cups or kids' choirs or fundraising announcements triggered paranoia about brainwashing and pyramid schemes. I couldn't seem to read the Bible without bumping into something I didn't like or didn't understand. Praying grew harder and harder, and I felt myself starting to give up.

Publicly, I grew obstinate and incorrigible, ready to debate family and friends whose easy confidence baffled and frustrated me and gave me an excuse to be angry at someone besides God. It bothered me that other people weren't bothered. I couldn't understand why no one else was stressed out about the existence of hell or angered by all the suffering in the world. I feigned surprise when my friends got annoyed that I raised such topics at bridal showers and poker games. Wherever I sensed a calm sea, I sought to rock the boat; I wanted others to share in my storm.

There's a chance this may have alienated me from some people.

Sarah seemed especially troubled. "Don't you think it's a little dangerous to be questioning God?" she asked one cold Saturday afternoon at Harmony House, the same coffee shop where I met with Nathan.

"Maybe it is," I said, warming my hands on my mug, "but I can't just snap my fingers and make these questions go away, Sarah. I'm really struggling with this idea that our eternal destiny is determined by luck of the draw, that most people go to hell simply for being born in the wrong place at the wrong time. Any way you look at it, that's unfair."

"People aren't damned because they don't know about Jesus," Sarah said. "They are damned because they are sinners. We are all enemies of God, Rachel. We all deserve hell."

"Yes, but if God is sovereign, then the fall was just a part of his plan. We're stuck with this sin nature that we can't control, and God punishes us for it. It's like we're just puppets on a string, and God is mad at us for doing what he makes us do."

Sarah looked ready to give up. "God's ways are higher than our ways, Rachel. At some point you have to accept the fact that you cannot understand everything he does. He is the potter. You are the clay. The clay can't tell the potter what to do."

"You know what, Sarah? I'm starting to wonder if maybe we made this potter up."

It was one of the last conversations she and I ever had about God. Even now, when we get together to catch up, we tend to talk around him the way people talk around a shared secret or a dead friend. I think we're both afraid of saying something wrong.

While some friends declared my faith dead on arrival, others insisted on defibrillation via systematic theology. Most insistent was my friend Andy,[8] who sent me an email with the subject line "just checking in" after hearing from someone (who heard from someone else) that I'd become a universalist, or a Buddhist, or something really terrible, like an Anglican. At the conclusion of the email, he wrote:

> I'm sorry to hear that a smart girl like you has become another cotton-candy Christian. I understand why you feel compassion for the damned, Rachel, but you can't let emotion and sentimentality determine your theology. Feelings cannot be trusted because feelings are perverted by our sin nature. Only God's Word can be trusted on matters like this.
>
> The truth is, God is utterly disgusted by our sin, and it is a miracle that he chooses to save any of us to begin with. Without him, we are vile and disgusting and worthy only of damnation. This notion that everyone is entitled to

salvation is a dangerous one, more reflective of culture's emphasis on individual rights than scriptural truths. None of us are worthy of God's grace, Rachel. I know that I am not. I encourage you to stop challenging God's sovereignty and consider taking a position of humility and thankfulness.

I'd heard this response many times before and had affectionately dubbed it "pond-scum theology." At the heart of pond-scum theology is the premise that human beings have no intrinsic value or claim to salvation because their sin nature makes them so thoroughly disgusting and offensive to God that he is under no obligation to pay them any mind. It's the view that inspired Jonathan Edwards' famed "Sinners in the Hands of an Angry God" sermon, in which Edwards told his trembling congregation, "The God that holds you over the pit of hell, much as one holds a spider, or some loathsome insect over the fire, abhors you, and is dreadfully provoked: his wrath towards you burns like fire; he looks upon you as worthy of nothing else, but to be cast into the fire; he is of purer eyes than to bear to have you in his sight; you are ten thousand times more abominable in his eyes, than the most hateful venomous serpent is in ours."[9]

It's a view recently resurrected by outspoken Reformed pastors who have argued that God can't even look at us because he is so disgusted by our sin nature, one even suggesting that God sent the tsunami to wash some of this pond scum from his sight. Pond-scum theology effectively shifts the question from How could a loving God send anyone to hell? to How could an angry God allow anyone into heaven?

While pond-scum theology provides an intellectually sat-isfying response to the problem of the unevangelized, it looks a lot better on paper than it does in real life, with real people who have real lives and real names. Pond-scum theology made sense in my head, but it never made sense in my heart. I knew that I was broken, that I was capable of great evil and tragically prone to sin, but deep down, at the very center of my being, I felt as though I still mattered to God. And I needed to know that Zarmina and Anne Frank mattered to him too. I needed to know that every person behind every pair of shoes recovered from every concentration camp mattered, that God had not for-gotten them, that he loved them, and that he knew each of their names. I needed to know that God does not make disposable people.

Pond-scum theology makes even less sense in the context of the Gospels. To believe that people are inherently worthless to God strips the incarnation, crucifixion, and resurrection of all their meaning and power. It makes Jesus look like a fool for dying for us, and it leaves his followers with little incentive to seek out and celebrate the good in one another.

When it came down to it, to believe that the reprobate are created for hell without any hope of salvation required that I ignore my most instinctive and visceral conceptions of right and wrong, good and evil, justice and love. I just couldn't stomach the idea that some people are beyond hope, that God has no intention of ever loving them, and that my compassion for them represented a weakness of faith. What Andy considered mere sentimentality and emotion, I considered the very essence of who I am. I can't just shut those instincts off. I don't want to.

I emailed Andy and told him I didn't like this version of God in which his wrath overwhelms his mercy, in which he has less compassion for people than I do.

"It's not my version of God," Andy wrote back. "It's God's version of God. Take it up with him."

———

Dan always says that as soon as you think you've got God figured out, you can bet on the fact that you're wrong. That's what he told me the following Sunday morning, as I lay curled up in a little ball in our bed, crying about how I'd rather that God just didn't exist than that he be so angry and vengeful and cruel.

He sat down next to me and ran his fingers through my hair. "Well, have you considered the possibility that maybe you're wrong?" he asked.

"You mean that God's ways are higher than our ways?"

"Well, sort of. What I mean is maybe you should look into the possibility that your issue isn't actually with God himself but with certain beliefs about him — you know, flawed ways of explaining him. Maybe you have misjudged God. Maybe he isn't this way at all."

"But the Bible says that God hates us and is going to send most of us to hell," I said, swallowing down tears.

"Does it?"

In the first few lines of *Traveling Mercies*, author Anne Lamott writes, "My coming to faith did not start with a leap but rather a series of staggers from what seemed like one safe place to another. Like lily pads, round and green, these places summoned and then held me up while I grew. Each prepared me for the next leaf on which I would land, and in this way I moved across the swamp of doubt and fear."[10]

My return to faith happened in much the same way, and this conversation with Dan represented the first little lily pad in my own journey across the swamp of doubt and fear. In the end, the same question that frightened and intimidated me as a child provided the clearest way out: What if I'm wrong? It was a question loaded with uncertainty, possibility, and hope, and it was a question to which I often would return. To be wrong about God is the condition of humanity, for better or for worse. Sometimes it lures us into questioning God; sometimes it summons us to give him another chance. After I'd thought for so many years that good Christians are always ready with an answer, it was a question that eventually drew me back to belief.

In the end, it was doubt that saved my faith.

CHAPTER 10

John the Revelator

Sometimes I think that John the Revelator might have been a crazy old man whose creative writing assignment for the Patmos Learning Annex accidentally made it into the Bible. There's a lot of strange stuff in the book of Revelation, stuff about dragons and "creatures full of eyes" and whores of Babylon and Middle Earth – style battles — the stuff people like to use to sell books about the end of the world and to launch websites about how Barack Obama is the Antichrist.

While I suspect that much of John's letter served as a coded allusion to the church's tumultuous relationship with the Roman Empire during the reign of Domitian, there's one apocryphal vision that I really hope he got right.

I bumped into it late one night after Dan had gone to sleep and I'd been awake for hours, worrying about what had happened to the hundreds of thousands of men, women, and children who perished in the Boxing Day tsunami. I couldn't force from my mind the haunting images of beautiful brown-skinned widows crying in agony as they clung to framed photos of their husbands and children, or the video footage of village after village lying in ruins from the unstoppable floods. Why would God allow something like that to happen in a part of the world where people had such limited access to Christianity? Didn't he promise never to flood the earth again? Had the population of hell just swelled to include the poor fishermen whose boats had overturned, the pregnant women who couldn't run fast enough to reach higher ground, the elderly who couldn't swim?

So, as I often do when I need to read but don't want to wake Dan, I grabbed my Bible from the nightstand, stumbled in the dark toward the bathroom, turned on the light, and sat on the toilet to await God's illumination of the text.

Normally, I wouldn't choose the book of Revelation as 2:00 a.m. reading material, but all night long I'd been chasing the broken pieces of a prophecy around in my head — something about tribes and tongues and nations, verses I knew but couldn't quite remember, like a poem with missing syllables or a song with forgotten words. After scanning John's messages to the churches at Ephesus, Smyrna, Pergamum, Thyatira, Sardis, Philadelphia, and Laodicea, I finally found what I was looking for in Revelation 7, where the author describes a world without a cosmic lottery, a kingdom in which the suffering are not forgotten. Writes John:

> I looked and there before me was a great multitude that no one could count, from every nation, tribe, people and language, standing before the throne and in front of the Lamb. They were wearing white robes and were holding palm branches in their hands. And they cried out in a loud voice:

"Salvation belongs to our God, who sits on the throne, and to the Lamb."... He who sits on the throne will spread his tent over them. Never again will they hunger; never again will they thirst. The sun will not beat upon them, nor any scorching heat. For the Lamb at the center of the throne will be their shepherd; he will lead them to springs of living water. And God will wipe away every tear from their eyes.

— REVELATION 7:9 – 10, 15 – 17

The passage reminded me of something Jesus said when one of his followers asked him, "Lord, are only a few people going to be saved?" After acknowledging that most of the people who encountered him in the flesh would simply follow the crowd and reject him as a radical, Jesus said, "People will come from east and west and north and south, and will take their places at the feast in the kingdom of God. Indeed there are those who are last who will be first, and first who will be last" (Luke 13:23, 29 – 30).

As I sat staring at the mustard-yellow tiles around our shower, I wondered what exactly John saw and heard to convince him that the kingdom of God includes people from *every* nation, tribe, people, and language, people from the north and the south and the east and the west. I imagined that he must have seen women wearing glorious red, green, and gold saris beneath their white robes. He must have seen voluminous African headdresses of every shape and color. He must have seen the turquoise jewelry of the Navajo, the rich wool of the Peruvians, the prayer shawls of the Jews. He must have seen faces of every shade and eyes of every shape. He must have seen orange freckles and coal-colored hair and moonlike complexions and the lovely flash of brilliant white teeth against black skin. He must have heard instruments of all kinds — bagpipes and lutes and dulcimers and banjos and gongs. He must have heard languages of every sound and cadence, melodies of every strain, and rhythms of every tempo. He must have heard shouts of praise to Elohim, Allah, and Papa God, shouts in Farsi and Hindi, Tagalog and Cantonese, Gaelic and Swahili, and in tongues long forgotten by history. And he must have seen the tears of every sadness — hunger and loneliness, sickness and loss, injustice and fear, tsunami and drought, rape and war — acknowledged and cherished and wiped away. In one loud and colorful moment, he must have witnessed all that makes us different and all that makes us the same.

Every now and then, we get lucky enough to catch a glimpse of the world as God sees it, a little revelation that gives us the hope to look beyond the confines of our current environment, be it exile or the bathroom. The fact is, while the Bible certainly speaks of God punishing the wicked, no single passage on judgment can compete with the scope and size of John's description of the redeemed. With this in mind, I returned to John's vision often, sometimes daily. Even on days when I wasn't sure that God exists, when I wasn't sure I loved him or even liked him much, I knew that I cherished this image of him. I don't know anyone, believer or skeptic, who doesn't long for a day when God wipes every tear from every eye, when "there will no longer be any death; there will no longer be any mourning, or crying, or pain" (Rev. 21:4 NASB). Even the faintest inkling that this might be true can keep you going for one more day.

Funny how after twenty years of sophisticated Christian education and apologetics training, I put my last best hope in the prophetic ramblings of an apocalyptic preacher.

CHAPTER 11

Higher Ways

As a kid, I never bought the line that all dogs go to heaven, but I was absolutely convinced that bullfrogs and butterflies do. We sang this song in children's church about how bullfrogs and butterflies have "both been born again," so I just assumed that God had bestowed upon them special salvific status within the animal kingdom. It took a while for me to figure out that the song was intended to be a metaphor illuminating the similarities between new life in Christ and the metamorphosis of insects and amphibians — pretty sophisticated stuff for the average seven-year-old, if you ask me.

Before I'd put all of this together, though, it occurred to me that if bullfrogs and butterflies could go to heaven, I didn't see why turtles couldn't go too. Amanda and I cherished fond memories of Herbie, a little box turtle we found sunbathing on a rock in our back yard one day and decided to make a pet. Herbie lived in an aquarium in Amanda's room, where we fed him grass and dog food until his habitat started to stink up the house and Mom insisted he be released back into the wild. She suggested we paint a little pink X on his shell with fingernail polish so we would know it was him should he ever wander back. Dad said he thought it unlikely that we'd ever see the poor chap again. He said he didn't even know turtles could run until he released Herbie from his shoe box that day. Anyway, it seemed to me that if for some reason Herbie didn't make it out there in the woods, he had as much a right as a bullfrog to die and go to heaven.

Justice has always been a big deal to me. I suppose all kids have a tendency to declare, "That's not fair!" when confronted with a perceived slight, but I probably said it more than most. I always checked to make sure Amanda and I had the same portion of ice cream in our bowls at snack time, the same amount of reading time with my father, and the same number of awards on our bedroom bookshelves. This heightened sensitivity to equality was undoubtedly influenced by my mother, who went to extraordinary lengths to make sure Amanda and I felt equally loved. To this day, she insists on making certain we have exactly the same number of presents under the Christmas tree each year.

Furthermore, both in word and deed, my mother taught us to look out for the little guy. She instructed us to give all of our classmates the benefit of the doubt, even the mean ones who probably came from "troubled homes." She encouraged us to invite the new students from school to our birthday parties and to send giant get-well cards made out of poster board to our friends with chicken pox. She spoke sympathetically about the bad kids, tenderly about the challenged kids, and warmly about the poor kids. She even stood up to teachers if she sensed they were picking on their students, once scolding my history teacher at a parent-teacher conference for assigning homework over spring break.

This is why whenever my mother and I go shopping together in town, kids run up to my mother and give her hugs and make a scene. Mom's fourth-grade classroom is the envy of Dayton City School because everyone knows she has this way of making each child feel like the most important person in the world. It's like she's got some sort of sixth sense that allows her to know all the things you secretly like about yourself so she can bring them up in front of people and make a big deal about them. It's wonderful. And it probably explains why I worry so much about what happens to people like Zarmina when they die and why Amanda works for nonprofit organizations that pay her peanuts to try to fix the world. We both seem to think that everyone deserves the chance to be loved.

Recently, a lot of good Christian people have tried to convince me that the compassion I inherited from my mother is a sort of spiritual liability, that when it comes to the eternal destiny of my fellow human beings, it's best just to accept without reservation the notion that most will be damned. "God's ways are higher than our ways," they say with a shrug. To demand that God meet human standards of justice reflects a childish preoccupation with fairness akin to eyeing the size of my sister's ice-cream scoop or insisting that turtles have the same rights as bullfrogs and butterflies.

For as long as I can remember, the assumption has been that the Bible speaks definitively about eternity, and that the news is not good for people like Zarmina. Born-again Christians go to heaven. Everyone else goes to hell. End of story. Those of us who lack the fortitude to accept God's Word on the subject are just "Burger King Christians." We want to "have it our way."

The problem for me is that such a scheme — which renders most people damned from the start based on geographical disadvantages — never sat well with my conscience, and my conscience is a big part of my faith. In fact, C. S. Lewis argued that the basic, intuitive sense of right and wrong written on every human heart serves as evidence for the very existence of God. He called this phenomenon the "moral law," and he used it to make a case for the reasonableness of faith. It seems to me that to ignore my conscience is to ignore the same voice that sings when I read the words of Jesus, that clears its throat when I'm about to do something wrong, that speaks against cruelty and oppression, and that shouts with every sunrise and every snowfall and every act of love, "Hey, God exists!" Apologists like to say that following Christ shouldn't mean checking our brains at the door. Perhaps it shouldn't mean checking our hearts either.

I faced an unnecessary ultimatum — believe the Bible or believe your conscience. Mercifully, before I could make my choice, I came upon another C. S. Lewis quote that changed everything.

"We do know that no person can be saved except through Christ," he wrote in *Mere Christianity*. "We do not know that only those who know Him can be saved by Him."[11]

I've never heard anyone call C. S. Lewis a "Burger King Christian."

Perhaps the most liberating moment in my journey from certainty to faith occurred when I discovered, as if for the first time, the diversity of my own religious tradition. In the time it took to accumulate about ten dollars in library fines, I learned that outside the tiny realm of conservative evangelicalism is a whole world of orthodox theology, a world in which there is more than one opinion about religious pluralism and the destiny of the unevangelized. From C. S. Lewis to Origen, Karl Barth to Karl Rahner, Clark Pinnock to Clement of Alexandria, theologians through the centuries have wrestled with and disagreed over the wideness of God's mercy. The Bible isn't as conclusive on the subject as I was taught. In fact, the more I studied, the more hopeful I became that John the Revelator wasn't as off his rocker as he seemed. Maybe his prophecy included people from every tribe, tongue, and nation because God really loves people from every tribe, tongue, and nation, and because the rest of Scripture supports such a claim.

God may determine when and where people are born, but according to Luke, he does not leave himself without a witness among them (Acts 14:17). God creates people in such a way that they might "seek him and perhaps reach out for him and find him, though he is not far from each one of us" (Acts 17:26 – 27). While the Bible teaches that people are justified by faith, it does not stipulate how much a person needs to know about God to be saved. It simply qualifies that the fruit of saving faith is good works. Paul writes that "it is not the hearers of the Law who are just before God, but the doers of the Law will be justified." People who have no knowledge of the Law but who "do instinctively the things of the Law" will be judged not on the basis of how much they know but on the basis of how they respond to their conscience (Rom. 2:9 – 16 NASB). We are not saved by information. We are saved by restored relationship with God, which might look a little different from person to person, culture to culture, time to time.

This explains why, throughout Scripture, we see evidence that God worked in the lives of people who were neither Jews nor Christians. Take, for example, Job, Abel, Enoch, Noah, Melchizedek, Abimelech, Jethro, the queen of Sheba, and the magi. The famed Hebrews 11 passage includes several of these so-called pagan saints in its elite "cloud of witnesses" (Heb. 12:1), emphasizing that they were saved by faith in a God who "is a rewarder of those who seek Him" (Heb. 11:6 NASB). When we require that all people must say the same words or subscribe to the same creeds in order to experience God, we underestimate the scope and power of God's activity in the world.

From the first covenant with Abraham to the vision of John at Patmos, salvation has always been described in terms of a blessing for the entire world, not just an exclusive privilege for a select group of people. The "election," first of Israel and then of the church, is not a spiritual condition but a vocational calling, a calling to serve the rest of the world, inviting others to join the kingdom of God. I cried tears of joy when I came across the apostle Peter's emotional response to the faith of a Gentile named Cornelius. Peter exclaimed, "I now realize how true it is that God does not show favoritism but accepts men from every nation who fear him and do what is right" (Acts 10:34 – 35).

I don't know exactly what this means for Zarmina, and I don't know exactly what this means for me. I don't know the degree to which God is present in the world's many religious systems. I don't know how God will judge the living and the dead. I don't know if hell is eternal or if God will destroy evil for good. I don't know what the new heaven and new earth will be like. I don't know if I'm an inclusivist or a universalist or a particularist. (They haven't made a Facebook quiz for that yet.) I don't know if I'll ever find the answers to all of my questions, no matter how much time I spend in the library. All I know is that if the God of the Bible is true, he loves his creation and will do whatever it takes to restore it.

This leaves me in an awkward position when it comes to always being ready with an answer. Gone are the black-and-white categories of "saved" and "unsaved," "heaven-bound" and "hell-bound." Gone are the old ways of determining who's in and who's out. Gone are the security of absolutism and the comfort of certainty. Gone is the confidence that comes with knowing that when Jesus said, "Not everyone who says to me, 'Lord, Lord,' will enter the kingdom of heaven," he of course couldn't possibly mean me.

But the assurance that I can still be a Christian without believing that God hates the world and damns most of it to hell gave me just enough hope to jump to the next lily pad on my way across the swamp of doubt.

It also made whatever money I owed the library totally worth it, so I stopped by the front desk late one evening to pay up, my purse heavy with the quarters I'd dug out of our change jar.

"Hmm," the librarian said, studying her computer. "Doesn't look like you owe anything."

"That can't be right," I said. "I'm pretty sure that *Four Views on Hell* is late because I found it under the seat of my car next to a bag of peanut brittle I got for Christmas."

"It says here that you don't owe anything," she said cheerfully. "Your fines must have been deleted when we updated the system."

It was like the Year of Jubilee.

I know Christians aren't supposed to say this, but there are some Bible verses that I don't like much. I don't like Psalm 137:8 – 9, where the writer says of Israel's enemies, "Happy is he who repays you for what you have done to us — he who seizes your infants and dashes them against the rocks." I don't like 1 Timothy 2:12, where Paul says to Timothy, "I do not permit a woman to teach or to have authority over a man; she must be silent." I don't like Joshua 6:21, where we find the story of how Israel attacked Jericho in the name of God and "destroyed with the sword every living thing in it — men and women, young and old, cattle, sheep and donkeys."

I used to feel the same way about Isaiah 55, because people always use the phrase "God's ways are higher than our ways" to explain why God sends earthquakes to Haiti, or why he finds glory in eternal torture, or why he makes fossils appear older than they are, or why he wants me to stop asking so many questions. I just assumed that Isaiah 55 spoke of God's terrible wrath against mankind, warning those who dare question his inscrutable ways to shut up and mind their own business.

So it came as a surprise when I went searching for God's higher ways and bumped into this:

> Seek the LORD while He may be found;
>> Call upon Him while He is near.
> Let the wicked forsake his way
>> And the unrighteous man his thoughts;
>> And let him return to the LORD,
>> And He will have compassion on him,
>> And to our God,
>> *For He will abundantly pardon.*
> "For My thoughts are not your thoughts,
>> Nor are your ways My ways," declares the LORD.
> "For as the heavens are higher than the earth,
>> So are My ways higher than your ways
>> And My thoughts than your thoughts.
> "For as the rain and the snow come down from heaven,
>> And do not return there without watering the earth
>> And making it bear and sprout,
>> And furnishing seed to the sower and bread
>>> to the eater;
> "So will My word be which goes forth from My mouth;
>> It will not return to Me empty,
>> Without accomplishing what I desire,

And without succeeding in the matter for which
    I sent it.
"For you will go out with joy
    And be led forth with peace;
The mountains and the hills will break forth into
    shouts of joy before you,
And all the trees of the field will clap their hands."

                —ISAIAH 55:6–12 NASB, ITALICS MINE

Where I expected to find anger, I found tenderness and affection. Where I expected to find a lecture, I found poetry. Where I expected to find God shaking his finger, I found trees clapping their hands.

Isaiah 55 provides an entirely different framework for thinking about God's justice, because it suggests that we have it backward — the mystery lies not in God's unfathomable wrath but in his unfathomable mercy. God's ways are higher than our ways because his capacity to love is infinitely greater than our own. Despite all that we do to alienate ourselves from God, all that we do to insult and disobey, God abundantly pardons again and again.

This is probably why, whenever Jesus spoke about forgiveness, he appealed to the character of God the Father as our model. In the Sermon on the Mount, Jesus said, "Love your enemies, and do good, and lend, expecting nothing in return; and your reward will be great, and you will be sons of the Most High, for He Himself is kind to ungrateful and evil men. Be merciful, just as your Father is merciful" (Luke 6:35–36 NASB).

We've got our way of dealing fairly with our enemies, and God has his. Our way involves retaliation and punishment; his way involves forgiveness. Our way involves equal justice; his way involves disproportionate grace. Our way is to make someone pay with blood; his way is to bleed. Even when Jesus hung on the cross, when God had been insulted to the highest degree imaginable, left naked, humiliated, beaten, and bruised, he said, "Father, forgive them for they know not what they do."

Now *that* is a higher way. *That* is the kind of goodness and grace my childish view of equality can never fully grasp. God's ways are higher than our ways not because he is less compassionate than we are but because he is more compassionate than we can ever imagine. When we forsake our way of doing things in favor of his, we experience the kind of joy and peace that inspires mountains to shout and trees to applaud.

What a comfort to know that this loving and merciful God will not be disappointed, that his word falls over the earth like rain, covers it like snow, and nourishes it for an abundant harvest. What a comfort to know that God is a poet.

CHAPTER 12

Laxmi the Widow

In recent years, it has become increasingly hip for restless Americans to travel to India in search of spiritual awakening. Most of us leave home with rudimentary understandings of Eastern religions, some newly acquired yoga moves, and the expectation of connecting with something fabulous and profound and worthy of a memoir before the end of the trip. We return smelling of curry and jasmine, with strings of sandalwood beads around our necks, henna all over our hands, and little amoebae swimming around in our stomachs.

When I boarded a plane to Hyderabad, India, in the fall of 2006, I was concerned more about losing my faith than finding it. The fact that religious pluralism initially triggered my faith crisis made a trip to the most religiously diverse country in the world seem more like a form of shock therapy than a vacation. But my sister, Amanda, had been in central India for three months, working with various ministries and nonprofit organizations there, and had invited me to join her for a few weeks as she transitioned to a new post in Bangalore. She needed the company, and I couldn't resist the opportunity to add an exotic stamp to my passport. We planned a cross-country trip that would take us from Hyderabad, to Delhi, to Agra, to Haridwar, to Rishikesh, and back to Delhi.

How folks manage to meditate in India is simply beyond me. From the first plaintive cries of the morning call to prayer, to the rhythmic swoosh and sigh of thousands of brooms across thousands of kitchen floors before breakfast, to the midday cacophony of cows mooing and roosters calling, vendors shouting and customers haggling, motorcycles roaring and bicycle bells chirping, to the distant beating of festival drums in the evening, the place never really quiets down. I spent the first few days dizzied by sensory overload, India's collage of colors and scents and sounds overwhelming me. I threw up a lot.

But as the days went by, my vision sharpened and I began to drink in the details one at a time: the way my sister's skin smelled like spices, the woman I spied brushing her teeth in the Ganges, the way the mist clings to the Himalayan foothills just like it clings to the Appalachians, the comfort of soft, sticky rice between my fingers, the pungent smell of garbage and excrement caught in a passing breeze, the gnarled hands of an old beggar on a crowded street, the way my rupees clinked when they fell into his tin cup. In India, everything is a picture. I took more than six hundred of them.

We spent the first week in Hyderabad, where Amanda taught English at a small residential school for children affected by HIV and AIDS. There I woke up every morning to the sound of dozens of little feet pattering on the floor above me and the sound of a woman named Laxmi making chapatis in the kitchen. Laxmi served as a caregiver at the school and a housekeeper for the Christian family that ran it. She rose before sunrise each day to make breakfast and wash the children's clothes. She rarely finished her duties until after dark. Slight, but not frail, Laxmi had a shy, dimpled smile and playful eyes. Although she spoke little English, she felt strangely familiar to me, like someone I knew as a child but couldn't quite place. Amanda and I learned to have conversations with her using only hand movements, facial expressions, and a few Telugu words. In all of my pictures of her, Laxmi is wearing a bright yellow sari with colored flowers around the edges, smiling demurely, shy of the camera.

Born in a rural village, Laxmi married at the age of seventeen and moved to the city, where she worked as housekeeper in several neighborhood homes. Soon after the birth of her third child, Laxmi's husband suddenly took ill, and tests revealed he was suffering from the advanced stages of HIV. This ostracized the family from the community and forced them to live on just one income. Before long, all five family members showed signs of severe malnutrition. Laxmi recalled overhearing whispers about how she and her youngest, little Latha, would certainly perish.

The Christians, who were native Indians themselves, took notice of the situation and offered to help Laxmi and her children get tested for the disease. Laxmi wept when she learned that both she and Latha were HIV positive. Her husband died a few months later.

Through a translator, Laxmi explained, "As a widow, especially an HIV-positive widow, my standing in society changed. I had no money, and I feared that my little daughter might not live to the age of five. At one point, I considered suicide. I knew it wouldn't be hard to give poison to Latha and take some myself, but because of my concern for the other children, I put that thought behind me."

The Christian family provided housing for Laxmi and her children and enrolled the little ones in school. Soon HIV patients from across the city and nearby towns were flocking to the home in search of help and advice. When the neighbors complained, the family held a public meeting educating the community about how AIDS is transmitted and prevented.

In India, children affected by HIV and AIDS are often denied an education, and widows are left destitute. Inspired by Laxmi's story, the Christian family opened a boarding school and offered widows job training and respectable positions in their ministry. When I was there, twenty-five children were enrolled in the school. Now there are more than thirty. All three of Laxmi's children attend, and thanks to sponsorship, little Latha receives the care she needs to stay healthy. Laxmi, who was raised Hindu, converted to Christianity. In between chores, she studies the Telugu alphabet, trying desperately to overcome illiteracy so she can read the Bible for herself.

By all accounts, Laxmi and the children at the school got completely screwed by the "cosmic lottery." If anyone has a right to complain, they do. It wasn't their fault that they were born in a country still heavily influenced by the caste system. It wasn't their fault that their husbands and fathers went to prostitutes. It wasn't their fault that they suffered from a disease so stigmatized and misunderstood that their own families often cast them out into the streets. And yet the widows and orphans I met in India were actually less angry with God than I was. In fact, they loved him in a way I couldn't quite understand.

Laxmi told me, "When I remember my life before HIV and compare it with how I am today, I am thankful. Were it not for my HIV, I never would have met Jesus. I never would have found salvation and hope."

For Laxmi, meeting Jesus had little to do with a transfer of information or a statement of belief and everything to do with outstretched hands offering food and shelter. In India, the gospel makes the most sense among the "untouchables," so many Christians choose to live in slums and among people suffering from leprosy, to take in the HIV-positive and the disabled, and to give generously to the poor. They subject themselves to poverty and earn reputations for associating with the lowest castes. They remind me of Jesus.

James, the brother of Jesus, once said that true religion is caring for orphans and widows, so I guess I shouldn't have been surprised when my first religious experience in India happened in the company of widows and orphans. About thirty of us were packed into a fifteen-passenger van, windows down, speeding down the streets of Hyderabad on our way to a church in the city. The kids, ranging in age from five to fifteen, were dressed in their Sunday best and were piled on top of one another, singing as loudly as possible and with no inhibition songs about Jesus in English and Telugu. My eardrums rang. My stomach lurched with every sudden swerve of the van. My lungs ached from inhaling pollution, and my head pounded from the heat.

But I hadn't felt that close to Jesus in years. I felt certain that he was crammed in there with us, singing along.

In India, I was introduced to the kingdom of heaven — not as it exists in some future state but as it exists in the here and now, where the hungry are fed with both physical and spiritual bread, where the sick are saved from both their diseases and their sins, where an illiterate widow taught me more about faith than any theologian ever could, and where children from the slums sing with God. In India, I learned that the gospel is still special. Jesus still matters and can make a difference in people's lives.

I guess that's close enough to spiritual awakening.

CHAPTER 13

God Things

Eight-year-old Kanakaraju looked up at me with dark, pleading eyes and tugged on my skirt. "*Akka, akka,*" he said urgently. *Akka* means "sister" in Telugu, and Indian children use it as a term of endearment.

I couldn't understand what Kanakaraju was trying to say, so I asked Amanda to translate.

"He's asking you to pray for his mother," Amanda said, pointing to the corner of the schoolroom, where a skeletal woman lay curled on the floor, a faded red and gold head scarf covering her face. I hadn't even noticed she was there.

"He wants you to pray for her to get better," she said. "Kanakaraju, can you say that to Rachel *akka* in English?"

Kanakaraju crinkled his brow in concentration. "*Akka,*" he finally said, "pray for my *amma* ... my mother ... please." A shy smile slowly spread across his face as Amanda praised him for listening so well in class.

Amanda explained to me that Kanakaraju's father had already died of complications caused by HIV, and things weren't looking good for his mother. Her death would leave Kanakaraju and his sisters orphaned.

I knelt and wrapped my arms around Kanakaraju's small body. He felt fragile, like a bird. "I will pray for your *amma*, Kanakaraju."

"Thank you, Rachel *akka*."

I hadn't been praying as consistently as I used to, but India changed how I did a lot of things, so I prayed for Kanakaraju and his mother every day. As I did, I realized just how petty and insignificant my typical prayer requests were in comparison. How could I ask God to heal me of a mild case of Delhi-belly when I'd seen children wading through garbage-chocked rivers, their ribs poking through their skin? How could I ask him to provide me with an air-conditioned hotel room when Kanakaraju's mother lay crumpled like a forgotten doll on a concrete floor?

After my return to the States, when my pastor asked the congregation to pray for the funds to repave the church parking lot, I privately asked God to take care of Kanakaraju's family first. It wasn't that I thought God was incapable of doing both. I guess I just figured that if prayer made any difference at all, it was more important that Kanakaraju have a mother than that my church have new blacktop.

But just a few weeks after I left India, I got an email from the missionary family saying that Kanakaraju's mother had succumbed to her illness. They planned to take Kanakaraju in themselves and start training his older sisters for sewing jobs so they could earn a living. The email said that Kanakaraju was struggling to accept his mother's death, that he was crying for her every night.

Not long after I got the message from India, my pastor announced that God had provided the funds for the parking lot.

"Isn't it amazing how God blesses his children?" he asked.

The first time I heard someone call something a "God thing" was in 2005, the Saturday after Hurricane Katrina hit. A friend of mine was getting married in Dayton and expecting family from all around the country to attend the wedding. At the reception, I spoke with a member of the family who expressed thankfulness that the entire family had made it to the ceremony, despite some major airport delays across the South.

"It was such a God thing," the young man said as we waited in line for a piece of the groom's cake. "It was like God had his hand on the weather. Clearly, he intends to bless this union."

I'd just spent the entire morning watching news footage of desperate families trapped on their rooftops awaiting rescue, so I couldn't help but bristle at what he said. God had his hand on the weather? If God had his hand on the weather, then why didn't he stop the hurricane from coming in the first place? Why didn't he keep the levees from breaking? Why would he go out of his way to help this family get to a wedding on time but leave thousands of people stuck in the Superdome without food or water?

Over the years, I've heard all sorts of things described as "God things" — scholarships, job opportunities, new cars, remodeled kitchens. Appealing to God things has an effect similar to appealing to "God's will." When a friend tells me that it's God's will for her to date a certain guy or buy a new car or go to a specific school, it's difficult to object or ask questions without looking like I want to pick a fight with the Almighty himself. Similarly, when my friend hails her low interest rate or her airfare or her concert tickets as a God thing, it's nearly impossible to get away with asking if she really needs a new house or a vacation or yet another Dave Matthews experience without seeming to rain on God's parade. Every good Christian knows that the best way to insulate yourself from criticism or input is to say that God wants whatever you want. It has been done for centuries, from Constantine's military conquests, to America's ethnic cleansing in the name of Manifest Destiny, to the televangelists' "love gifts."

Dan says I'm far too cynical. He says that Christians talk about God things in an effort to show sincere gratitude to God, to remind themselves and others that the good things in their lives are not earned or deserved but are gifts. After all, the Bible says that "every good and perfect gift is from above."

I tell him that I'm not convinced that boats and cars and stainless-steel kitchen appliances qualify as "good and perfect gifts."

Here he usually suggests that I tone down the snarkiness and consider tending to the massive log sticking out of my own eye before I start going at others with tweezers.

I know that he's right. I know that, deep down, my problem isn't really with Christians who celebrate their blessings but with a God who seems to bless arbitrarily. What bothers me about God things is that they remind me of the cosmic lottery — that sobering dichotomy between the world's rich and the world's poor, between the lucky and the unlucky — which has always been a sticking point in my own fitful walk with God. If God's goodness is qualified by how much stuff he gives out, I reason, then he's not especially good. He might be good to that family that made it to the wedding on time, but he's not especially good to orphans like Kanakaraju.

I couldn't quite piece it together at the time, but in India, I began to suspect that perhaps the problem lies not in God's goodness but in how we measure it. Laxmi and Kanakaraju and the women and children at the AIDS ministry, they prayed for basic things — food, shelter, health, peace — and they did not always receive. Yet I saw in their eyes the kind of joy and spiritual connectedness that most Christians I know long for. They spoke of Jesus like one speaks of an intimate friend or lover, as if they had just returned from a long walk by his side, their faces still flush from the movement, their breathing still labored from trying to keep up. The children, though robbed of much of their childhood, showed no sense of entitlement. The women, though burdened, displayed unfailing strength.

Maybe we aren't the lucky ones after all.

Once, when he was eating with a group of religious leaders, Jesus told a fascinating story:

A certain man was preparing a great banquet and invited many guests. At the time of the banquet he sent his servant to tell those who had been invited, "Come, for everything is now ready."

But they all alike began to make excuses. The first said, "I have just bought a field, and I must go and see it. Please excuse me."

Another said, "I have just bought five yoke of oxen, and I'm on my way to try them out. Please excuse me."

Still another said, "I just got married, so I can't come."

The servant came back and reported this to his master. Then the owner of the house became angry and ordered his servant, "Go out quickly into the streets and alleys of the town and bring in the poor, the crippled, the blind and the lame."

"Sir," the servant said, "what you ordered has been done, but there is still room."

Then the master told his servant, "Go out to the roads and country lanes and make them come in, so that my house will be full. I tell you, not one of those men who were invited will get a taste of my banquet."

—LUKE 14:16 – 24

From the start of his ministry, Jesus had a special relationship with the poor and the oppressed. He even singled them out as special recipients of the gospel, saying, "The Spirit of the Lord is on me, because he has anointed me to preach good news to the poor. He has sent me to proclaim freedom for the prisoners and recovery of sight for the blind, to release the oppressed, to proclaim the year of the Lord's favor" (Luke 4:18 – 19). It is impossible to read the Gospels without noticing that the sick, the downtrodden, the ostracized, and the marginalized were always the first to respond to Jesus' invitation to join him at the banquet table of a new and strange kingdom, what he called "the kingdom of God."

While earthly kingdoms belong to the rich and powerful, Jesus spoke of a kingdom that belongs to the meek and the gentle, the merciful and the peacemakers. Whereas earthly kingdoms usually start with a sovereign leader taking control, Jesus said his kingdom would start small, like a mustard seed, and grow from the bottom up. While earthly politicians associate with the rich and elite, Jesus associated with outcasts. While earthly kings prefer liberty by conquest, Jesus spoke of liberty through forgiveness.

Perhaps most disconcerting for those of us who enjoy relatively affluent lifestyles, Jesus said that his kingdom is more accessible to the poor than to the rich. "It is easier for a camel to go through the eye of a needle," he said, "than for a rich man to enter the kingdom of God." When his disciples protested, asking, "Then who can be saved?" Jesus responded by saying, "What is impossible with men is possible with God" (Luke 18:25 – 27). (You can get that last part printed on a canvas tote bag for twenty-one bucks online.)

It seems that in the kingdom of heaven, the cosmic lottery works in reverse. In the kingdom of heaven, all of our notions about the lucky and the unlucky, the blessed and the cursed, the haves and the have-nots are turned upside down. In the kingdom of heaven, "the last will be first, and the first will be last" (Matt. 20:16).

In India, I realized that while the poor and the oppressed

certainly deserve my compassion and help, they do not need my pity. Widows and orphans and "untouchables" enjoy a special access to the gospel that I do not have. They benefit immediately from the good news that freedom is found not in retribution but in forgiveness, that real power belongs not to the strong but to the merciful, that joy comes not from wealth but from generosity. The rest of us have to get used to the idea that we cannot purchase love or fight for peace or find happiness in high positions. Those of us who have never suffered are at a disadvantage, because Jesus invites his followers to fellowship in his suffering.

In fact, the first thing Jesus did in his Sermon on the Mount was to mess with our assumptions about the cosmic lottery. In Luke's account, Jesus says,

> "Blessed are you who are poor, for yours is the kingdom of God.
> Blessed are you who hunger now, for you will be satisfied.
> Blessed are you who weep now, for you will laugh....
> But woe to you who are rich, for you have already received your comfort.
> Woe to you who are well fed now, for you will go hungry.
> Woe to you who laugh now, for you will mourn and weep."
>
> —LUKE 6:20–21, 24–25

It seems the kingdom of God is made up of "the least of these." To be present among them is to encounter what the Celtic saints called "thin spaces," places or moments in time in which the veil separating heaven and earth, the spiritual and the material, becomes almost transparent. I'd like to think that I'm a part of this kingdom, even though my stuff and my comforts sometimes thicken the veil. Love, joy, peace, patience, kindness, goodness, faithfulness, gentleness, and self-control — these are God things, and they are available to all, regardless of status or standing. Everything else is just extra, and extra can be a distraction. Extra lulls us into complacency and tricks us into believing that we need more than we need. Extra makes it harder to distinguish between "God things" and just things.

In another interesting reversal of the cosmic lottery, Jesus seems to give the spiritual edge to the nonreligious over the religious. This is not especially good news for someone who won the Best Christian Attitude Award four years in a row.

If the poor were the most receptive to Jesus and his message, then the religious were the most repelled by it. They benefited too much from the status quo to tolerate the radical teachings of Jesus, so they tested him with trick questions, criticized him for hanging out with sinners, and ultimately helped arrange for his crucifixion. The Pharisees in particular pestered Jesus constantly. When he healed the sick, they attacked him for doing it on the day of rest. When he ate and drank with his friends, they called him a glutton and asked why he didn't fast as often as they did. When he offered forgiveness for sins, they called him a blasphemer. When he taught, they questioned his credentials. When he cast out demons, they claimed he did it with Satan's help. Once, when Jesus healed a lame man and instructed him to pick up the pallet to which he had been confined for years, the Pharisees actually chastised the poor guy for carrying a heavy object on the Sabbath! No wonder Jesus repeatedly said to the highly educated Pharisees, "Go and learn what this means: 'I desire compassion, and not sacrifice'" (Matt. 9:13 NASB).

The irony is that of all the first-century Jews, the Pharisees knew best what to look for in the Messiah. They had combed the Scriptures for years, searching for clues about his arrival. But as Jesus marveled to Nicodemus, the religious folks just didn't seem to get it. They were so confident in their own interpretations and expectations that they missed the fulfillment of Scripture altogether, so convinced they already had God figured out that they didn't recognize him in the flesh. To the Pharisees, Jesus just didn't fit the mold. His theology was too edgy, his friends too salacious, and his love too inclusive.

In return, Jesus publicly criticized the Pharisees for being hypocritical and self-righteous. He warned his followers against imitating them and stressed the condition of the heart over outward acts of righteousness and sterilized, airtight orthodoxy. Jesus told the Pharisees that the tax collectors and prostitutes would get into the kingdom of heaven before them. Imagine the surprise of the people when Jesus said that in his kingdom, their righteousness could surpass that of the Pharisees.

I'm afraid that just as wealth and privilege can be a stumbling block on the path to the gospel, theological expertise and piety can also get in the way of the kingdom. Like wealth, these are not inherently bad things. However, they are easily idolized.

The longer our lists of rules and regulations, the more likely it is that God himself will break one. The more committed we are to certain theological absolutes, the more likely we are to discount the work of the Spirit when it doesn't conform to our presuppositions. When we cling to our beliefs as children cling to their favorite toys, it is hard for Jesus to take us by the hand and lead us somewhere new.

In a surprising prayer, Jesus says, "I praise you, Father, Lord of heaven and earth, because you have hidden these things from the wise and learned, and revealed them to little children. Yes, Father, for this was your good pleasure" (Matt. 11:25 – 26).

When I'm honest with myself, I have to admit that the people I most identify with in all of Scripture are the Pharisees. Like the Pharisees, I know a lot about the Bible and am familiar with all the acceptable -isms and -ologies of orthodoxy. Like the Pharisees, I am skeptical of spiritual movements that don't conform to my expectations about how God works in the world. Like the Pharisees, I like to try to cram the Great I AM into my favorite political positions, theological systems, and pet projects. Like the Pharisees, I am judgmental, crave attention, and fear losing my status as a good believer.

It is natural for most Christians to assume that had we lived in Galilee two thousand years ago, we would have dropped everything we owned and followed Jesus. But I'm not so sure that those of us with expensive Christian educations and deeply religious backgrounds would have fallen in line. I'm beginning to suspect that most of us would have joined the Pharisees and enrolled in the I Hate Jesus Club.

Jesus drank wine with sexual deviants. He committed major social taboos. He spent a lot of time among contagious people, crazy people, uneducated people, and smelly people. His famous cousin wore camel hair and ate locusts and honey. Those most familiar with Scripture called his views heretical, and his own family questioned his sanity. Jesus introduced new teachings not found in the Scriptures and claimed his authority came directly from God. He asked his disciples to sell all their "blessings" and follow him, when doing so could get them excommunicated from the faith or even killed. He was too liberal, too radical, and too demanding. To tell you the truth, I'm not sure that I would have followed the guy, and that really scares me sometimes.

Fortunately for us Pharisee types, Jesus offers hope in the form of his conversation with Nicodemus. Nicodemus was himself a Pharisee and a member of the prestigious Sanhedrin. He had a lot of questions for Jesus and seemed a bit skeptical, but Jesus assured Nicodemus that if he was willing to start all over again, willing to let some things go and think a little differently, he could experience this new kingdom himself. Jesus said to him, "I tell you the truth, no one can see the kingdom of God unless he is born again" (John 3:3). (You can get that printed on a bumper sticker for just a dollar.)

In India, I learned that among Hindus, the goal of reincarnation is to be reborn into nobler circumstances. And in India, I learned that in the kingdom of God, the goal is to be reborn into humbler ones.

CHAPTER 14

Mark the Evangelist

Mark started his lecture the same way he always did, by snapping his fingers slowly and rhythmically, like a ticking clock.

Snap. Snap. Snap.

He didn't say anything. He just snapped.

Snap. Snap. Snap.

The sharp, loud clicks reverberated off the walls of the chapel, where several hundred high school students waited nervously for Mark to speak.

Snap. Snap. Snap.

Finally he paused, scanned the room solemnly, and asked, "Did you know that every second, seven people die?"

Snap. Snap. Snap.

"That means twenty-one people just passed into eternity."

Snap. Snap. Snap.

"By the time you put your head on your pillow tonight, six hundred thousand people will have walked off planet Earth and stood before the throne of Almighty God."

Snap. Snap. Snap.

"How many of them will go to hell?"

Snap. Snap. Snap.

"More important, *do you care*?"

Snap.

A former college basketball player with an imposing six-foot-seven frame, Mark traveled the country, asking questions like these of Christian college students and church youth groups. He spoke with captivating intensity, punctuating each sentence with conviction, as if pounding a gavel. He shared stories about his life as an evangelist and described how he witnessed to strangers at public parks and sporting events, in airports and on airplanes, at shopping malls and bars, to waitresses, salespeople, postal workers, pedestrians. He taught the Way of the Master technique (made popular by Kirk Cameron on TBN), in which the proselytizer approaches a person in a public place and asks if the person obeys all of the Ten Commandments. If the person admits to breaking just one of the commandments, the evangelist uses the opening to explain how sin separates us from God and how the only way to restore relationship with him is to embrace Jesus as Savior. Failure to do so results in a one-way ticket to hell.

"How many of you have witnessed to someone within the last twenty-four hours?" Mark asked. "Raise your hands."

A palpable awkwardness fell over the auditorium as one or two people (who I suspected were fibbing) raised their hands.

I suspected they were fibbing because the first time I heard Mark speak, I fibbed a little myself. I was in high school at the time and a few weeks earlier had witnessed to my lab partner in biology class. I figured that no one else in my youth group ever would have done something that brave, so I went ahead and raised my hand even though it hadn't technically happened within the past twenty-four hours. I soaked in Mark's approving glance, only to feel a wrenching twinge of guilt after he looked away. I'd just broken one of the Ten Commandments.

This time, as a young adult with a seat in the balcony and a little less to prove, I didn't raise my hand.

"That's not right," Mark said as he surveyed the meager response from the students. "That's just not right.

"Let me ask you something," he said. "How many of you believe that hell is a real place?"

A few people in the auditorium murmured "amen."

"If you believe hell is a real place, then the question isn't, How *can* you share your faith? but, How can you *not* share your faith?" Mark said. "The two most important questions you will ever ask yourself are these: One, Do you know where you are going when you die? And two, Who are you taking with you? Once you die, there is no turning back. You are either in heaven or in hell, and you will be there forever and ever and ever and ever. The question for those of you who are born again is, Who will be there with you? You've got extra tickets to heaven in your pocket, and you've got to hand them out now because you can't cash them in after you die."

Mark went on to share some anecdotes about people who had near-death experiences that involved fire and wailing and that sort of thing. He implied that born-again Christians have good near-death experiences, but everyone else has bad near-death experiences. (I'd seen enough Barbara Walters specials to know this isn't true.) He then offered some pointers for witnessing to people who believe in the theory of evolution, which he described as having "absolutely no evidence to back it up." (I'd seen enough of the Discovery Channel to know that isn't true either.)

"Let me ask you something," Mark said as the clock approached 11:50. "How many of you are happy to be alive?"

The students sensed this was a test, so the applause was hesitant.

"Sure beats the alternative, right?"

The room fell silent again.

"Folks, the apostle Paul said, 'To live is Christ and to die is gain.' I've got news for you: death beats life. If your dream is to be with Jesus, then death beats life. The problem is, you're too distracted by the stupid, pointless things of life to care about eternity. You're too distracted by homework and ball games and parties to make sure you're witnessing for Christ."

"Every second, seven people die."

Snap. Snap. Snap

"Will you be the next to go?"

Snap. Snap. Snap.

"Or will it be your neighbor?"

Snap. Snap. Snap.

"Who's going to stand up for God today?"

Snap. Snap. Snap

"And who's going to let him down?"

Snap.

CHAPTER 15

Judgment Day

Every October, as the days grow shorter and the hills light up with color, talk in East Tennessee revolves around two things: football and soul-saving. While communities across the region open corn mazes and host bluegrass festivals to draw tourists from the city, churches in Dayton and nearby towns prepare their annual Judgment Day houses. In contrast to regular haunted houses designed to scare teenagers into one another's arms with trap doors, fake blood, and mirrored hallways, Judgment Day houses are designed for a higher purpose: to scare people into getting saved.

Judgment Day committees spend months planning such events. Signs outside churches count down the days, "Ten Days until Judgment: Are You Ready?" As the various opening nights draw near, congregations transform the inside of their buildings into elaborate sets designed for walk-through dramas about heaven and hell. Heaven is generally located in the sanctuary, where Christmas lights strung across the ceiling represent stars and white sheets draped over the pews represent clouds. Hell often occupies the basement, its dark, narrow hallways leading to a fellowship hall lined with red and orange bulletin-board paper shaped like flames.

Making the annual pilgrimage to the local Judgment Day house was as much a part of my high school experience as homecoming or prom. The Sunday before Halloween, my friends and I joined hundreds of our classmates at a nearby church, where the drama, though slightly different each year, played out in essentially the same three acts.

Act 1 takes place in the sanctuary, which will later be transformed into heaven while the rest of us are in hell. The lights dim, and a spotlight shines on one corner of the stage, where four actors (usually members of the youth group) sit in a car without windows or doors for the classic "driving back from prom" skit.

The driver (the partier) informs the group of his intentions to get high and have sex with his girlfriend. His girlfriend (the airhead) giggles and agrees that this is a splendid idea. The guy in the back seat (the moral kid) objects, saying he can't indulge in sex and drugs because he intends to earn his way into heaven through works of righteousness. His girlfriend (the born-again Christian) agrees but explains that if you accept Jesus Christ as your personal Lord and Savior, you will have everlasting life, regardless of good works. Unfortunately, before she can lead her friends down the Romans Road, we hear a loud car-crash, and the spotlight suddenly goes out. We shift nervously in our seats, waiting for the next scene.

The spotlight then shines on four caskets (generously donated by the local mortician), which are surrounded by the teens' friends and families, who spend the next few minutes discussing the fragility of life and marveling about how something so terrible could happen on prom night. The light cuts out again, and a disembodied voice instructs us to head downstairs for act 2.

We leave the sanctuary quietly and follow a solemn deacon into the basement. The church must spend a fortune on heating each October, because the whole place is always burning-hot for effect. The deacon introduces us to the Angel of Death (the local orthodontist), who is dressed in black pants, a black turtleneck, and a black fedora. The Angel of Death leads us silently through dark hallways, where strobe lights make everything move in slow motion. Youth group members wearing ski masks are hiding behind the doorways of Sunday school classrooms, waiting to jump out and startle us. "Satan's legions welcome you!" they shout. A Halloween sound-effects CD, complete with screams, organ music, and maniacal laughter, plays in the background.

Somehow we all manage to cram into an incredibly warm fellowship hall, which is glowing like a lava lamp from all the red filters placed over the lights. In the center of the room is a raised platform, where we see three of the four teenagers from act 1 — the partier, the airhead, and the moral kid. The moral kid is, of course, shocked to find himself there, seeing as he'd done so many good works in life. A bunch of demons circle the three and taunt them. Then one of the demons points her finger dramatically to the back of the room and says, "Behold! The Prince of Darkness!" Satan (usually the church youth leader) makes his grand entrance. Wearing a pinstriped suit, leather gloves, and a black trench coat, he glides toward the platform, nudging demons and audience members with an ornate cane (generously donated by a local antiques collector).

"Please!" shouts the airhead as he approaches. "Let us out of here!"

"I can't do that," Satan says in a sinister voice. "You've already made your choice."

He joins the three onstage.

"But what about all the works of righteousness that I did in the name of God?" asks the moral kid. "Don't they count for anything?"

Satan laughs hysterically. "That's one of my favorite tricks," he says, eyeing the audience carefully, "convincing people that they are saved by good works."

"Then how can I be saved?" asks the moral kid.

"It's too late now," Satan says before calling on his legion to take the three away and throw them into the lake of fire (a curtained puppet stage in the corner of the fellowship hall). Each teen is pushed into the flames until only their hands remain visible, reaching out toward the audience in desperation. The demons dance around and celebrate their demise. It's quite dramatic.

The Angel of Death then leads the hushed crowd back upstairs and into the sanctuary again for act 3. The rush of cool air provides a welcome relief after the 85-degree hell, with its strobe lights and bad sound effects. Contemporary Christian music hums in the background as volunteers wearing white sheets line us up to form a big circle around the church. Pretty much everything in the auditorium is covered up with white sheets — the pews, the communion table, the baptismal font, even the lectern. Yellow bulletin-board paper lines the aisles to symbolize streets of gold, but it sticks to the bottom of our shoes, which seems to stress out some of the angels who had so painstakingly laid it down before we got there. Candelabras (generously donated by the local wedding supply shop) adorn the stage, where we see the born-again Christian standing with Jesus. You know he's Jesus because he's wearing the most professional costume of the night, a white robe with bell sleeves and an attached crimson shoulder drape. You also know he's Jesus because the same deacon plays Jesus every year, probably on account of his stunning blue eyes.

Jesus holds an enormous unabridged dictionary, which is meant to be the Book of Life. He looks for the born-again Christian's name, and sure enough, there it is.

"Well done, my good and faithful servant," Jesus says loudly, so everyone can hear. "Welcome to the kingdom of heaven."

Someone turns the music up louder as Jesus goes down the line and pats each one of us on the back, saying, "Well done, my good and faithful servant," his breath smelling of Tic Tacs. At this point, the adult chaperones start to cry, making us all feel a little embarrassed and awkward. The room starts to feel too cold, and my friends and I shift uncomfortably on our tired legs, tearing little holes in the streets of gold. This part always seemed to take forever, and I remember wondering once if I really wanted to spend the sweet by-and-by shivering and listening to Avalon.

Finally, the pastor arrives to present the plan of salvation and conduct an altar call.

"The Bible says that God wants to save you from hell," he says at the conclusion of his remarks. "All you have to do is believe in Jesus as your Savior and you can go to heaven. It's that simple."

Usually, several hundred kids committed (or recommitted or re-recommitted) their lives to Jesus as a result of the Judgment Day house. Unfortunately, most of them turned into what my friends and I came to call "Judgment Day Christians," new believers who spent about a week dutifully abstaining from sex and alcohol but inevitably returned to their previous lifestyles without much change in their behavior or outlook on life. I can't say I blame them. After all, the pastor had gone to great lengths to remind everyone that good works don't really count for anything, that choosing to live like Jesus did was something we could do for extra credit but didn't matter much in the long run. Living like Jesus was important, but it had no saving power.

Most Christians I know have had some kind of Judgment Day experience. It might have been a skit at summer camp, a puppet show at vacation Bible school, or a dramatic encounter with someone like Mark in a chapel service or on a street corner. When you grow up in church, however, these events tend to lose their impact over time, as the thrill of making your reservations for eternity wears off and you start to wonder what being a Christian means for the day-to-day. Even those of us who tried to "walk the walk" by going to discipleship groups, starting Bibles studies, and evangelizing got bored with our Christianity every now and then. Sometimes it just seemed like all we were doing was killing time.

The first thing I learned about heaven was that you can't get there in roller skates. According to the song we sang in children's church, you'll roll right by the pearly gates doing something crazy like that. Don't try a limousine, a car, or a boat either, because as it turns out, the only way to get to heaven is through Jesus.

This seemed simple enough to me as a child. Jesus was a part of everyday life. We talked to him at lunch and dinner and before bed, sang songs about him in children's church, watched cartoons about him getting born in the manger, and colored pictures of him rising from the dead. It never occurred to me not to believe in Jesus. It would be like not believing in Abraham Lincoln or gravity. As soon as I was old enough to be aware of death, I was certain of eternal security. I knew that Jesus had given me a ticket to heaven, and I intended to cash it in someday. In fact, my mother used to tease Amanda and me by singing, "Heaven is a wonderful place, filled with *joy* and *grace*," tickling us when we recognized our middle names: Amanda Joy and Rachel Grace. Heaven indeed sounded like a wonderful place, where, I imagined, I would stroll the streets of gold without having to look both ways, where, I imagined, no one ever cried or got sick or had bad skin.

Like a lot of kids who grew up in church, my salvation was of no concern to me until I learned about hell. The first thing I learned about hell was that it is a terrible place. The second thing I learned was that a lot of people are going to be surprised to find themselves there. I learned all of this by accident one Wednesday night when I was about six years old. All the other kids were at AWANA, but I stayed back with my parents for "Big Church" because I had a stomachache. Mom let me rest my head on her lap, and I listened to our pastor explain how important it was to know for sure that you trusted Jesus for your salvation, because if you didn't, you would spend eternity separated from God, in hell: a place of fire, torment, and despair. He said that because we are all sinners, we deserve to go to hell, but thanks to Jesus' dying on the cross, we could go to heaven anyway. We just had to accept his death as atonement for our sins.

So that was the top-secret information they discussed in Big Church while the rest of us snacked blissfully on apple juice and animal crackers! I knew that I was a sinner, and I knew that Jesus had died on the cross to save me from my sins, but I had no idea that getting saved from my sins meant getting saved from this place called hell. Suddenly, simply coloring Jesus in a coloring book didn't seem like enough. I needed to be sure that I got this thing right. I needed to be certain that my ticket into heaven was valid, because the last thing I wanted was to go to hell when I died.

We went to a Bible church, so we never had any altar calls like the Baptists, but I don't think I would have gone forward had there been one. I felt embarrassed, as if I'd just learned a dirty word: *hell*. I imagined it as a long, hot tunnel of darkness with sticky linoleum floors where people constantly wept and where children were offered candy by sinister strangers who smoked and used the Lord's name in vain.

I waited until later that night, when my parents came into my room to pray with me, to make my move. I told them that I didn't want to go to hell and that I wanted to be sure I was a Christian. They told me not to be afraid and talked with me for a while about Jesus. I told God that I accepted the forgiveness of Jesus, adding at the end of my prayer, "And thank you for letting me go to heaven," just to make sure we were square. I suppose this was the moment of my conversion, although it didn't seem to me that much had changed. I didn't love Jesus any more than I already had loved him, and I suspected that he had always loved me too. But I felt better now that I'd crossed the t's and dotted the i's when it came to something as important as eternity.

By age ten, I was well acquainted with the conversion process. I knew that when my Sunday school teacher asked me and my fellow students to bow our heads and close our eyes, souls were about to be won to Jesus. I was thankful that I'd asked Jesus into my heart in the safety of my own bedroom, because most of the other kids had to raise their hands while the rest of us pretended not to look. I always peeked through my fingers to see who would be joining me in heaven. That's how I discovered that Mr. Andrews, my AWANA leader, said, "God bless you," even when no one raised their hand.

Some of my friends weren't as confident as I, which led to a host of rededications during Bible camp in the summer. I remember that poor Sammy Martin rededicated his life to Jesus every single year, and I felt so sorry for him, because he didn't need to be afraid of losing his salvation. Once your name was written in the Book of Life, Satan couldn't just come along with some giant eraser and take it out. "Once saved, always saved," we liked to say. But Sammy was one of those kids who lived in constant terror of getting unsaved, so every year, he marched his way to the front of the rustic little chapel at Bible camp and rededicated himself to Jesus, while the rest of us pretended to keep our eyes closed.

Christians have been obsessed with the afterlife for centuries. From the weird, teeming landscapes of Bosch's triptychs to Michelangelo's glorious tones of light and flesh and sky, artists have spent ages trying to capture the horror and splendor of the afterlife of popular imagination. Dante envisioned nine concentric circles of hell, where the damned are tortured in accordance with their sins, a "Mountain of Purgatory" that had seven terraces corresponding to the seven deadly sins, and nine celestial spheres of heaven. Today, books describing near-death experiences that include firsthand encounters with bright lights and beautiful music, hellfire and the scent of sulfur, soar to the bestseller list. Mercy Me's hit song "I Can Only Imagine," which celebrates the hope of eternal worship before the throne of God, became one of the most requested songs of the year in 2003. My own doubts about Christianity centered around conflicted feelings about heaven and hell as I struggled to reconcile God's goodness with his wrath.

It hasn't always been this way. In fact, for the writers of the Jewish Scriptures, details concerning the afterlife were murky. Solomon wrote that "the living know that they will die, but the dead know nothing; they have no further reward, and even the memory of them is forgotten" (Eccl. 9:5). Job knew only that after death, "the wicked cease from turmoil, and ... the weary are at rest" (Job 3:17). He later asked, "If a man dies, will he live again?" (Job 14:14). Although David claimed that God would redeem him from the power of sheol, he had no promise of mansions, pearly gates, or a crystal sea in return for faithfulness. For the children of Israel, the essence of religion was experiencing God to the fullest during this lifetime, not merely preparing for the next.

Sometimes I try to imagine what my life would be like if I had grown up assuming that I could experience God only within the parameters of this present world. I wonder if I would look more closely for him in the simple, everyday things, if I would ask more questions and search harder for the answers, if I would be seized by a sense of wonder and carpe diem, if I would live more deliberately and love more recklessly. Sometimes I wonder if this is why the Bible talks about Seth, Methuselah, and Jared living for more than eight hundred years. Maybe they just wanted more time with God.

By the time Jesus came along, most Jews had embraced the concept of resurrection, and by this they envisioned a physical resurrection of the body, not some floating away of a disembodied soul. Most anticipated the resurrection of God's people into a future kingdom of justice and peace. Jesus didn't say much to change this perspective. However, his own resurrection provided a powerful, tangible example of the future bodily resurrection of all, a phenomenon the apostle Paul described as "the firstfruits of those who have fallen asleep" (1 Cor. 15:20). In other words, Jesus set the stage for what was to come.

Consequently, the focus of the early church was not on the state of one's soul immediately after death but rather on preparing for a new kingdom here on earth, a kingdom that Jesus had embodied and talked about and shown them how to create, a kingdom to which God's people would someday be resurrected, a kingdom in which the veil between the physical world and the spiritual world would evaporate to make every space a "thin space." The seeds for this kingdom were already being planted among the poor, the peacemakers, the merciful, and the gentle, and one day Jesus would return to bring it to fruition.

N. T. Wright, the bishop of Durham for the Church of England, has written extensively on this subject, and his books were influential in helping me rethink my approach to heaven. In *Surprised by Hope*, he writes, "God's kingdom in the preaching of Jesus refers not to postmortem destiny, not to our escape from this world into another one, but God's sovereign rule coming 'on earth as it is in heaven.' … Heaven, in the Bible, is not a future destiny but the other, hidden dimension of our ordinary life — God's dimension, if you like. God made heaven and earth; at the last he will remake both and join them together forever."[12]

According to Wright, participants in the early church understood that the ultimate goal wasn't to die, leave their bodies behind, and float around like ghosts in heaven forever but rather to embody, anticipate, and work toward a new kingdom. What happened to a person in between death and resurrection remained a bit of a mystery, although the apostle Paul assured his fellow Christians that "to be absent from the body" is "to be present with the Lord."

N. T. Wright made me wonder if perhaps I'd missed the point. Perhaps being a Christian isn't about experiencing the kingdom of heaven someday but about experiencing the kingdom of heaven every day. Perhaps I could get a little taste of what the Old Testament saints thought was worth sticking around for.

I used to think that being saved from my sins meant being saved from hell. Salvation was something that kicked in after death, like a gift that had "Do not open until eternity" on the tag. To "get saved" meant to make an intellectual commitment to the deity of Christ and the theology of substitutionary atonement in order to avoid the wrath of hell. It was something that happened once but applied for all of eternity — once saved, always saved.

From this perspective, Jesus was little more than a theological deus ex machina, a vehicle through which my eternal security was attained. As my Sunday school teacher used to say, "Jesus was born to die." The whole point was for Jesus to act as a sacrifice on my behalf. Everything that happened between the manger and the cross was interesting but not necessary. It had no inherent saving value. Jesus was like the conductor who handed me my ticket for heaven but left me alone for the ride.

I think this is why people always ask me, "If non-Christians can receive salvation, then what is the point of Jesus? Why did he die on the cross, and why should we bother to share the gospel?" They assume that the gospel is important only when it saves people from hell. They assume that Jesus' purpose was simply to alter the afterlife.

Laxmi is a good example of why the gospel matters regardless of one's position on religious pluralism. When Laxmi encountered Jesus Christ through the kindness and compassion of his followers, it wasn't just her eternal destiny that changed; her entire life was transformed into something new. She found relationship with God. She found a community. She found hope and peace. When Laxmi encountered Jesus, she was saved not just from the eternal ramifications of sin but from the ugly everyday ramifications of sin: the caste system, poverty, despair, anger, victimization, worry, and fear. Just because I think God will be merciful when he judges doesn't mean I think the gospel is pointless. I believe the gospel is the most important thing in the world! It should be shared no matter what.

Jesus came to offer more than just salvation from hell. I realized this when I encountered Jesus the radical rabbi and reexamined my life in light of his teachings. When I imagined what it would be like to give generously without wondering what is in it for me, to give up my grudges and learn to diffuse hatred with love, to stop judging other people once and for all, to care for the poor and seek out the downtrodden, to finally believe that stuff can't make me happy, to give up my urge to gossip and manipulate, to worry less about what other people think, to refuse to retaliate no matter the cost, to be capable of forgiving to the point of death, to live as Jesus lived and love as Jesus loved, one word came to mind: *liberation*. Following Jesus would mean liberation from my bitterness, my worry, my self-righteousness, my prejudices, my selfishness, my materialism, and my misplaced loyalties. Following Jesus would mean salvation from my sin.

What I'm trying to say is that while I still believe Jesus died to save us from our sins, I'm beginning to think that Jesus also lived to save us from our sins. The apostle Paul put it more eloquently in his letter to the church in Rome when he said, "For if, when we were God's enemies, we were reconciled to him through the death of his Son, how much more, having been reconciled, shall we be saved through his life!" (Rom. 5:10).

If it's starting to sound like I believe in works-based salvation, it's because I do. While I don't for one second think we can earn God's grace by checking off a to-do list, I do believe that there is liberation in obedience. When we live like Jesus, when we take his teachings seriously and apply them to life, we don't have to wait until we die to experience freedom from sin. We experience it every day as each step of faith and every good work loosens the chains of sin around our feet. It's hard, and it's something that I fail at most of the time, but it's something I've experienced in little fits and starts along the way, enough to know that it's worth it. Jesus promises that his yoke will be light, because he carries most of the load.

I never know what to say when a street preacher in the parking lot of Shop Rite asks me if I'm saved.

"Saved from what?" I usually ask.

"Saved from your sins," he will say.

"Well, I guess I'd have to say that Jesus and I are working on that."

I always leave with extra tracts stuffed in my purse.

CHAPTER 16

Adele the Oxymoron

I first met Adele on my blog, when she posted a really smart comment using the screen name Existential Punk. I followed a link to her site, where she described herself in her profile as being "a doubter, a betrayer, a traveler … redeemed by the grace and beauty of God." That was enough to convince me that we had a few things in common, so Adele and I struck up a little friendship on the blogosphere.

I'd always wanted a gay friend. But, as embarrassing as this is to admit, I wanted the sort of gay friend who would give me fashion advice and add some diversity to my clique, the kind of gay friend who would make me look edgy and open-minded, not the kind who would actually challenge my thinking or stereotypes.

As a fellow writer and friend, Adele inspired me to reexamine some of my assumptions. The more we talked, the more I learned about what life is like for gay and lesbian people who are followers of Jesus. The more I learned, the less I felt I knew. The less I felt I knew, the more I listened.

"People tell me that I'm an oxymoron," Adele said in an email.

"They tell me that I have to choose between being gay and being a Christian, that I can't be both."

Adele grew up in a moderately religious home in Cincinnati, where she attended a private Catholic school. Even as a child she had crushes on other girls, but she repressed those feelings in order to fit in. As a sophomore in college, Adele responded to an altar call at a conservative charismatic church. Her born-again experience led her to attend a Christian graduate school in Virginia Beach, where she fell into an on-again, off-again physical relationship with another woman. Counselors told Adele that the relationship had to end because it violated Scripture.

"That's when I determined to try to pray away the gay," she says. "I got involved in an ex-gay ministry where the purpose was to heal me of my homosexuality so that I could attain the ideal — marriage to someone of the opposite sex. I attended conferences where I received anointing oil and splashes of holy water. I bought mountains of books and tapes. I fasted and prayed. I begged God to heal me, but no miracle occurred. I felt like a failure. I became deeply depressed and tried to kill myself, which twice landed me in a psychiatric hospital for over a month. It's not that I really wanted to kill myself; I just didn't want to live this awful life. Sometimes I self-mutilated by hitting myself because I seethed with so much loathing and disgust for myself. No matter how hard I tried, I couldn't change."

After struggling through counseling, Adele moved to Los Angeles, where she lived a double life, pretending to be straight around her Christian friends while secretly pursuing gay relationships on the side. It wasn't until her thirties, Adele says, that she made peace with both God and her sexuality. She blogs about her experience on a site called *Queermergent.*

"For a long time I despised God and the Bible," Adele told me. "The Bible has always been used as an excuse to treat me with hatred and revulsion."

I thought about the signs I've seen at protest rallies on TV, signs that say things like "Turn or Burn: Luke 13:3," or "AIDS Is the Cure: Romans 6:23," or "God Hates Fags: Genesis 19." I could see why opening the Bible might make someone like Adele wince.

Sometimes when I want to put myself in Adele's shoes, I imagine an alternate universe in which Christians have chosen different biblical stones to throw, condemning women who uncover their heads or people with tattoos. I imagine TV preachers claiming that 9/11 happened as a result of God's wrath on the gossipers and the greedy, and churches raising funds to support an amendment to the constitution making remarriage illegal for people who are divorced. I imagine people carrying signs that say "God Hates Gluttons" or "Stone Disobedient Children" or "Shellfish Are an Abomination." When it comes to Scripture, we tend to pick and choose in ways that are favorable to our own interests.

That's when I realize that if anyone's an oxymoron, it's me. Or maybe it's anyone who claims to follow Jesus.

Sword Drills

When I was a little girl, I knew I could be anything I wanted to be when I grew up, except a pastor. According to my Sunday school teacher, the Bible says that only boys can grow up to lead churches. I didn't find this particularly disappointing at the time, as I planned to be either an author or a cowgirl when I grew up, and the Bible doesn't have anything to say about that. But the whole thing bothered me a little bit because it made me feel like God had reserved all of the important, spiritual jobs for the boys, like he thought that girls are second best.

Once when I saw a lady preacher on TV, I asked my dad if he thought she would go to hell. He said he didn't think so, so I asked him if he agreed with my Sunday school teacher that only boys could grow up to be pastors. "Well, I think that's what the Bible teaches," he said. "But some people disagree with me on that." The lady on TV wore a fuchsia suit, white stockings, and black heels. She had a short haircut and a throaty Southern accent. For some reason, she upset me. I felt as though she had disturbed my paradigm somehow.

I quickly learned that to grow up as a strong-willed woman

in the conservative evangelical community is to never quite understand your place in the world. It means sorting through a barrage of mixed messages from both male and female authority figures regarding your proper role in society, the church, the home, even the bedroom, each message punctuated by the claim that it is God's will that you do this or that. I'm not sure when I first encountered the concept of "biblical womanhood," but I've spent most of my life trying to figure out what that means, wanting desperately to be the kind of woman God wants me to be.

The hermeneutical mazes can be dizzying. Women cannot be pastors, I learned, because in a letter to Timothy, the apostle Paul said he did not allow women to teach or exercise authority over men (1 Tim. 2:12). These instructions apply to all women at all times and in all cultures. However, the apostle's admonition just two sentences before, that women should not braid their hair or wear expensive clothes (1 Tim. 2:9), no longer applies literally but is culturally constrained. In fact, it was good if I looked especially nice at church, just not so nice that I made my brothers in Christ stumble. I learned that while Paul encouraged mutual submission in his letters to early churches, women are the only ones specifically defined by this role and should therefore defer to their husbands when it comes to decision making in the home. Churches that encouraged women to pursue traditional gender roles in compliance with 1 Timothy 2 were "Bible-believing" churches, but those that required women to cover their heads in compliance with 1 Corinthians 11 were "legalistic." I learned that I should try to model myself after the virtuous woman described in Proverbs 31, who rose before dawn and worked until dark managing the home. (She also had servants, a fact that usually went unmentioned.) God prefers women in supporting roles as helpers, I learned. Biblical women such as Miriam, Deborah, Huldah, and Phoebe — who served as prophets, teachers, judges, and leaders — were counted as anomalies and largely ignored. No one talked much about Mary for fear of coming across as too Catholic.

I was always disconcerted by the inconsistencies in biblical interpretation and confused about what all of this meant for me. When boys didn't volunteer for leadership positions in my youth group, I took them on myself, to the warm praise of members of my congregation. Once when I spoke in church about the AIDS crisis (violating 1 Cor. 14:34, which states that women should remain silent in the churches), I received only the kindest of compliments and encouragement. A friend of mine once told me, "You'd be a great preacher if you were a guy." So I always found myself pushing the boundaries a little bit — leading Bible studies among both male and female peers, running for student government positions in college, writing and speaking on biblical topics, and pursuing a career before starting a family. People rarely complained. In fact, my leadership qualities were often affirmed and celebrated, and for that I was incredibly thankful, though a little perplexed.

The whole concept of "biblical womanhood" really began to unravel for me at apologetics camp. The goal of the conference was to teach teenagers and young adults to adopt a Christian position on every conceivable issue — science, economics, politics, the role of men and women in society — based solely on the Bible. My job was to guide a group of seventeen-year-old girls through the material at the end of each day, answering any questions they might have.

On the day we discussed gender roles, the speaker explained that the Bible serves as the single authority regarding matters of church, state, and home. Women should therefore take their cues from Scripture, as God's Word contains everything we need to know about gender identity. Feminism was decried as an abomination and blamed for societal ills such as divorce, consumer debt, and unruly children. At the mention of Hillary Clinton, the room erupted with groans and snickers from the audience. The speaker said that when it comes to dating, the Bible includes some clear guidelines. Among them are waiting until we are financially ready for marriage before pursuing romantic relationships, abstaining from sex until marriage, dating only in the presence of friends and family to avoid tempting situations, deferring to parents on dating decisions, and honoring God-ordained gender roles in preparation for married life. For men, this means assuming the role of leader in the relationship. For women, it means stepping back to allow men to take the lead.

Some of the teenage girls in my group were understandably mystified by such a scheme. Later that night, one of the girls nervously confessed that she had invited a boy to prom, thereby inadvertently usurping his God-ordained leadership role in their relationship. Another, a soft-spoken, pretty red-haired girl with an easy demeanor, buried her head in hands, ashamed of having kissed a boy. Their responses embodied all that I felt as a young woman trying to find my way in the conservative religious culture — the shame, the confusion, the sense that my sexuality and ambition were liabilities in my relationship with men and with God.

I didn't know what to say to them then, but if I could somehow go back, I know what I would say to them now. I would tell them not to be ashamed, that God loves them just as they are and isn't angry at them for wanting to take on the world as powerful women. I would tell them that to claim there is a biblical view of dating is a bit of a stretch, since people in the Bible didn't date. I would tell them that using the Bible as a model for marital relationships requires some selectivity, seeing as how in Bible times women were generally sold by their fathers to the highest bidders, men were free to take as many wives as they pleased, and women who had been raped could be required to marry their rapists. I would tell them that the idea of a single, comprehensive biblical worldview to which all Christians can agree is a myth and that it's okay to ask questions about people's interpretations. I would tell them that this doesn't diminish the beauty and power of the Bible but rather enhances it and gives Christians something to talk about. And I would tell them that womanhood, like the Bible, is far too lovely and mysterious and transcendent to systematize or explain.

One of my most vivid memories of my childhood is of sitting on my hands in a folded metal chair, the buckles of my white

Mary Janes clinking frantically against its legs. I wait with my classmates for Miss Linda to deliver the command. My Bible sits closed on my lap, but it feels alive with tension, as if it might jump out at any moment. The room is silent and still, despite being filled with nearly a dozen twelve-year-olds who have just been served a generous amount of apple juice.

Miss Linda clears her throat.

"Romans 3:23!" she finally shouts.

First comes the sound of little hands against leather-bound books, then the rustling of paper, then the panicked whispers of "3:23, 3:23, 3:23," then impatient groans as some of us get lost rushing backward through the Epistles. After about twenty seconds, someone jumps out of his chair and triumphantly shouts, "For all have sinned and fall short of the glory of God!" as if he's just discovered a cure for cancer or something.

Following an unenthusiastic spattering of applause and sighs, some congratulations from Miss Linda, and a few complaints about how so-and-so knocked so-and-so's Bible out of so-and-so's hands, the room falls silent again so the process can start over.

"Keep your hands off your Bible until I give you the verse," Miss Linda reminds us before shouting, "First Timothy 3:16!"

Sword drills were my introduction to the world of competitive Bible-verse finding. Named from the passage in Ephesians 6 in which the apostle Paul instructs his readers to put on the full armor of God, sword drills were designed to help familiarize young soldiers with the basic layout of the Bible, which is described by the apostle as the "sword of truth." I got pretty good

at sword drills over the years. A cornerstone activity at vacation
Bible school and AWANA, these drills prepared me for years of
personal study and corporate readings. Sometimes when I'm sitting in church and the pastor instructs the congregation to turn
to a certain passage, I eye the people around me and then rush
to beat them to it. I like winning pointless little games like that.

For as long as I can remember, the Bible has been compared to a weapon, and for as long as I can remember, it has
been used as one. Many of us who participated in sword drills
as kids never really grew out of them. We just learned to adapt
the overall technique to more adult circumstances, like theological debates, political positions, or confrontations with other
Christians. Rather than using the whole Bible as a sword, however, we tend to pick out certain verses and use them as daggers
so we can fight at closer range. We take short, frantic stabs at
each other — a John 10 from the soldier for limited atonement, a
1 John 2 from the soldier for unlimited atonement, an Isaiah 66
in the name of God's wrath, an Isaiah 55 in the name of his
mercy. These battles usually leave us bloody and scathed and
angry but rarely mortally wounded or dramatically changed.
Occasionally, opposing forces will unite to fight against easier
targets, shooting arrows from Matthew 5 at the divorced and
dropping bombs from Leviticus 18 on gays and lesbians.

Only in the battles over biblical inerrancy do the weapons
of mass destruction surface. The best way to silence an opponent in biblical warfare is to question his or her commitment to
an error-free Bible. This usually happens to me after I've gone
and said something like, "Maybe Genesis 1 is not meant to be

a scientific explanation of how the world began," or, "I think Paul's instructions for the Corinthian church are culturally constrained," or, "I don't like that verse and am not sure what to make of it."

"Are you saying that you don't believe the text is inerrant?" someone inevitably will ask.

"No, I'm saying that I don't think your interpretation is inerrant," I'll respond defensively.

"Oh, so you think that *your* interpretation is without error?"

"Well, no … I suppose I could be wrong."

"So then whose interpretation is inerrant?"

The dense silence that falls between us is enough to make us realize that we have just come upon something important, something that could potentially change everything, something that could result in the demise or rebirth of Christianity, something infinitely more frightening and intriguing and life-changing than anything we have encountered before, and yet something entirely beside the point.

There is an exchange of troubled glances, an eerie quiet on the battlefield, and then the fighting resumes.

The Bible is by far the most fascinating, beautiful, challenging, and frustrating work of literature I've ever encountered. Whenever I struggle with questions about my faith, it serves as both a comfort and an agitator, both the anchor and the storm. One day it inspires confidence, the next day doubt. For every question it answers, a new one surfaces. For every solution I think

I've found, a new problem will emerge. The Bible has been, and probably always will be, a relentless, magnetic force that both drives me away from my faith and continuously calls me home. Nothing makes me crazier or gives me more hope than the eclectic collection of sixty-six books that begins with Genesis and finishes with Revelation. It's difficult to read a word of it without being changed.

The apostle Paul wrote that Scripture is "inspired by God," and yet it is clear that the Bible has human handprints all over it. The Bible is perfection crammed into imperfect language, the otherworldly expressed in worldly ways, holiness written down by unholy hands, read by unholy eyes, and processed by unholy brains. Filled with poetry and history, laws and letters, stories and genealogies, the Bible is commonly referred to as "God's Word," a description that sounds so definitive and singular that it is almost misleading. In truth, the Bible represents a cacophony of voices. It is a text teeming with conflict and contrast, brimming with paradox, held together by creative tension.

For a skeptic like me, the Bible is at times helpful and at times troublesome. On the one hand, I love what Jesus said about forgiveness and enemy love. On the other, I am horrified by the acts of genocide committed by Joshua in the Old Testament, acts seemingly condoned, even ordered, by God. While I marvel at Christ's embrace of the poor and suffering and his unorthodox appreciation for women in a patriarchal culture, I struggle to accept what can be described only as misogynistic elements in biblical stories and law: how women were assumed to be responsible for infertility, how Paul said that women are more easily deceived than men, how no one objected to polygamy or the kidnapping of virgins as spoils of war. It baffles me that the same God who cast the lepers out of Israel sent his Son to minister among them. The same God who ordered the death of every man, woman, and child in Canaan welcomed little children into his arms. I wonder why Jesus, in a radical move, chose women to be the first witnesses to his resurrection, only for Paul to omit them from his account for fear of sounding unreliable. In the Bible, there are passages that speak of God's unsurpassed wrath and passages that speak of his unfathomable mercy, verses that describe his love as universal and verses that describe his love as territorial, stories in which he is hailed as uncompromising and stories in which he changes his mind. All my life I've been taught that the Bible is the glue that holds Christianity together, so whenever I encounter parts of it that don't make sense, I start to worry that my faith might fall apart.

When I am among fellow Christians, my questions are usually met with dismissive confidence — "That was part of the old covenant, of course," or, "This is clearly meant to be interpreted poetically," or, "That's just from the Old Testament," or, "Jesus obviously was speaking hyperbolically." Occasionally, someone will come right out and say, "What's the big deal anyway? Why can't you just get over it?" or, "Shhhh … the movie's starting." If I've learned anything about what it's like to be on the outside of Christianity looking in, it's how awful it feels when your questions aren't taken seriously. Sometimes I just want to hear someone say, "You know, I'm not sure what to make of that either."

Invariably, I will be referred to Gleason Archer's massive

Encyclopedia of Bible Difficulties, a heavy volume that seeks to provide the reader with sound explanations for every conceivable puzzle found within the Bible — from whether God approved of Rahab's lie, to where Cain got his wife. (Note to well-meaning apologists: it's not always the best idea to present a skeptic with a five-hundred-page book listing hundreds of apparent contradictions in Scripture when the skeptic didn't even know that half of them existed before you recommended it.)

Despite all of the elaborate explanations and rationalizations, all the theological justifications and hermeneutical treatises, most Christians are offended by the accusation that they "pick and choose" from Scripture. Now, this is an issue I can relate to from both perspectives, that of a believer and that of a skeptic. To the skeptic, it's complete nonsense: "Of course you pick and choose; you're okay with people eating shellfish, but you're not okay with women teaching in church." But to a lot of believers, it's perfectly reasonable: "Yes, but I have good reasons for interpreting the Bible differently in different circumstances; there's a method to my madness, and it's called hermeneutics."

The skeptic may rightly point out that it's mighty convenient for a passage condemning other people's actions to be taken literally, while a passage condemning one's own actions should be ignored.

I think the truth lies somewhere in the middle. I know for a fact that a lot of my Christian friends have thoughtful reasons for interpreting the Bible the way they do and that the phrase "pick and choose" sounds far too arbitrary to describe the attentiveness and concern with which they approach the text. I don't like it when people tell me that I "pick and choose," especially when I feel that I've spent a lot of time studying and contemplating an issue. On the other hand, I'm also convinced that our interpretations of the Bible are far from inerrant. The Bible doesn't exist in a vacuum but must always be interpreted by a predisposed reader. Our interpretations are colored by our culture, our community, our presuppositions, our experience, our language, our education, our emotions, our intellect, our desires, and our biases. My worldview affects how I read the Bible as much as the Bible affects my worldview. In fact, I'd say that how I interpret the Bible (or how I "pick and choose") says as much about me as it says about God.

Here's what I mean: There's this mysterious passage in the Gospels in which Jesus says, "Do not give dogs what is sacred; do not throw your pearls to pigs. If you do, they may trample them under their feet, and then turn and tear you to pieces" (Matt. 7:6). When I was Reformed, I assumed this referred to the nonelect. When I was Arminian, I assumed it referred to the unrepentant. When I voted Republican, I thought it might refer to welfare moms, people leeching off the system. When I voted Democrat, I thought it might refer to the powerful and elite. When I was a fundamentalist, I was convinced it referred to liberal Christians. When I was a social justice advocate, I was convinced it referred to conservative ones. At the moment, I'm inclined to think the passage refers to literary critics. You can tell a lot about someone based on who they fear might tear them to pieces.

This is why I've grown increasingly skeptical that there is such a thing as a biblical worldview. When we refer to "the biblical approach to economics" or "the biblical response to politics" or "biblical womanhood," we're using the Bible as a weapon disguised as an adjective. We inadvertently imply that embracing the Bible as truth requires embracing one interpretation of it. This results in false fundamentals, which result in an inability to change, which results in a failure to adapt and evolve. Imagine if geocentricism were still "the biblical view of cosmology"!

In his book *Velvet Elvis*, pastor Rob Bell writes, "In Jesus' world, it was assumed you had as much to learn from the discussion of the text as you did from the text itself. One person could never get too far in a twisted interpretation because the others were right there giving her insight and perspective she didn't have on her own. Jesus said when he was talking about binding and loosing that 'where two or three come together in my name, there I am with them.'"[13]

Sometimes I wonder who really had the most biblical support back in the 1800s, Christians who used Ephesians 6 to support the institution of slavery, or Christians who used Galatians 3 to support abolition. Both sides had perfectly legitimate verses to back up their positions, but in hindsight, only one side seems even remotely justifiable on a moral level. On the surface, the Bible would seem to condone slavery. But somehow, as a church, we managed to work our way around those passages because of a shared sense of right and wrong, some kind of community agreement. Maybe God left us with all this discontinuity and conflict within Scripture so that we would have to pick and choose for the right reasons. Maybe he let David talk about murdering his enemies and Jesus talk about loving his enemies because he didn't want to spell it out for us. He wanted us to make the right decisions as we went along, together. Maybe God wants us to have these discussions because faith isn't just about being right; it's about being a part of a community.

For as long as I can remember, the Christian response to conflicts within Scripture has been to try to explain them away, to smooth over the rough spots and iron out the kinks. The goal is to get everyone on the same page, to come up with one consistent, coherent, and comprehensive biblical worldview so that we can confidently proclaim that God indeed has an opinion about everything, including politics, economics, theology, science, and sex. We think that if we can just have a perfect, seamless book that can be read objectively and without bias, we will have the ultimate weapon. There will be no need for a God who stays hidden up on Mount Sinai, and there will be no need for each other. Instead, we will have a physical representation of God on which to dwell, personal idols made of paper and ink.

As much as I struggle with the things I don't like about the Bible — the apparent contradictions, the competing interpretations, the troubling passages — I'm beginning to think that God allows these tensions to exist for a reason. Perhaps our love for the Bible should be measured not by how valiantly we fight to convince others of our interpretations but by how diligently we work to preserve a diversity of opinion.

I've had the same Bible since junior high. My maiden name is engraved on the front in loopy gold letters that look tiny and shy against the black leather cover. The corners are folded, the spine frayed, and many of its pages so severely corrugated that words look distorted and crammed together, as if passing under a dimpled glass. I can't bring myself to get a new one. I've grown so familiar with all of its irregularities and markings that I have trouble finding my way around other Bibles. It serves as a diary of sorts, a spiritual travelogue told in sloppy underlines and barely legible notes, notes that I hastily scribbled in the margins with markers in high school, ink in college, and pencil more recently.

At first, I felt embarrassed about having my name on the cover. It seemed presumptuous, as if I were taking credit for something. But now I'm glad it's there. It means I can never open my Bible without being aware of my own presence beside it. It reminds me that I'm always there, that I cannot read a word of this glorious, God-breathed book without bringing myself along, baggage and all. All that I think of when I think of my name — my memories, my secrets, my culture, my education, my opinions, my relationships, my sexuality, my prejudices, my preferences, my sincerest hopes, and my deepest fears — colors and infuses and brings to life everything that I read. My interpretation can be only as inerrant as I am, and that's good to keep in mind.

PART 3

CHANGE

CHANGE

CHAPTER 18

Sam the Feminist

L ike me, Sam asked questions for a living, only she was much better at it.

We worked together in the newsroom, sharing leads, discussing politics, cheering each other through tight deadlines, and complaining about how they paid us peanuts for slave labor. With her extra twenty years of experience, Sam helped me navigate through the insider's world of local politics and taught me how to gently, but persistently, work the story out of a reluctant source. She smoked during her lunch break, smarted off to the editor now and then, and used her nickname in bylines because she said readers took her more seriously when they thought she was a man. While I liked to bury the lead, Sam always got right to the point.

I'd cut my journalistic teeth at a city newspaper in Chattanooga, where I noticed that as soon as word got out that I'd graduated from a conservative Christian college, my coworkers stopped swearing around me. They also stopped inviting me to lunch. But I met Sam at the Dayton paper, where, as a self-described "washed-up Commie," she was the odd one out among her conservative colleagues. Despite our political differences at the time, we shared a dry sense of humor and an aversion to male-dominated power structures and soon became good friends and allies in the newsroom.

Sam worked the county beat, so she was one of the first to report on the Rhea County Commission's controversial resolution to charge gays and lesbians with crimes against nature.

"I just don't see how a smart girl like you can be one of them," she said one day, looking at her computer monitor.

"One of what?" I asked.

"One of those evangelicals," she said.

"Well, not all evangelicals think homosexuality should be illegal," I said. "In fact, I'd say that most evangelicals in this town weren't too happy about that commission decision."

"Oh, I know," she said, looking over her glasses at me and studying me with her quick, brown eyes. "But it's just that attitude — you know, that blind certainty that they can't be wrong about anything."

"Maybe if you got to know more Christians you wouldn't think that," I said. "Maybe if you came to church with me sometime — "

Sam released a deep, breathy laugh.

"Let's see," she said. "I'm a Democrat, I'm a feminist, and I have gay friends. Something tells me I wouldn't fit in with the church crowd."

I realized that she was probably right but tried again anyway.

"You might be surprised," I said. "I mean, it's not like you *have* to be a conservative to be a Christian."

Sam laughed so hard that she started to cough. "Well, maybe

someone ought to tell the Christians that," she finally said, "or Karl Rove, for that matter."

Sensing my disappointment, she added, "Listen, I respect you and your commitment to your faith. Really, you're one of the nicest Christians I know. It's just that I've had some pretty nasty run-ins with your conservative evangelical cohorts and I don't think I'm cut out for that lifestyle. I'm not into all the hellfire and damnation stuff, and I'm definitely not into this submit-to-your-husband stuff. I can't imagine telling my gay friends that they've got to force themselves to be straight, and I can't imagine voting for a guy like Bush just because he's pro-life. Now, I've got no problem with Jesus. But it seems to me that if evangelical Christians were the only ones to have God all figured out, then they would be the kindest, most generous people around. No offense to you, but in my twenty-plus years in this business, I haven't found that to be true. Most Christians I know are only interested in winning arguments, converts, and elections."

I should have been ready with an answer, but I wasn't. The truth was, I thought Sam was right. Somewhere along the way, the gospel had gotten buried under a massive pile of extras: political positions, lifestyle requirements, and unspoken rules that for whatever reason came with the Christian territory. Sometimes Jesus himself seemed buried beneath the rubble.

"I know what you mean," I said. "I'm sorry that the church doesn't look more like Jesus."

"Oh, honey, it's not your fault," Sam said. "It's probably just because it's run by men."

This time we both laughed.

CHAPTER 19

Adaptation

It's always a little embarrassing when you come out swinging and there's nobody there to fight with you. I think that's how a lot of us felt when we realized that the world wasn't asking the questions we had learned to answer. Many of us who grew up in the church or received Christian educations were under the impression that the world was full of atheists and agnostics and that the greatest threat against Christianity was the rise of secular humanism. But what we found upon entering the real world was that most of our peers were receptive to spiritual things. Most believed in God, were open to the supernatural, and respected religious ideas so long as they were not forced upon them. Most were like Sam. They weren't searching for historical evidence in support of the bodily resurrection of Jesus. They were searching for some signs of life among his followers.

Not once after graduating from Bryan was I asked to make a case for the scientific feasibility of miracles, but often I was asked why Christians aren't more like Jesus. I may have met one or two people who rejected Christianity because they had difficulties with the deity of Christ, but most rejected Christianity because they thought it means becoming judgmental, narrow-minded, intolerant, and unkind. People didn't argue with me about the problem of evil; they argued about why Christians aren't doing more to alleviate human suffering, support the poor, and oppose violence and war. Most weren't looking for a faith that provided all the answers; they were looking for one in which they were free to ask questions.

Before long, those of us who were supposed to be ready with the answers started asking questions too. As we encountered new cultures and traditions, it became harder and harder to convince ourselves and others that evangelical Christians in America had a monopoly on absolute truth. Some of my friends who were raised to despise Roman Catholicism, for example, felt suddenly drawn to the tradition's beautiful liturgy and its appreciation for historical Christianity. Others who had been taught that mainline Protestants were too liberal found their commitment to social justice refreshing, if not essential to the faith. Many of us who had once considered religions like Buddhism to be one-dimensionally evil were finding spiritual enrichment in practicing mindfulness and yoga. We'd gone from a world in which the United States was the only big player to one in which multiple countries were contributing to a colorful and vibrant marketplace of ideas. The assumption that God belongs to a certain country, political party, denomination, or religion seemed absurd.

My generation is perhaps more equipped than any other to defend the uniqueness of Christianity, but we are also the most capable of seeing things from a different perspective. So we began to deconstruct — to think more critically about our faith, pick it apart, examine all the pieces, and debate which parts are essential and which, for the sake of our survival, we might have to let go. Within a three-year period, my faith changed dramatically, and I sensed I was not alone. I sensed that the cultural climate was changing and that other people of faith were probably asking some of the same questions that I was asking. So, like any good, self-aware millennial, I started a blog.

I called it *Evolving in Monkey Town*, and I wrote about the process of trying to figure out which parts of my faith are fundamental and which are not. Before long, a little online community developed, and as the comments rolled in, so did the survival stories. Some people had struggled with religious pluralism, others with the Bible. Some had questions about homosexuality, others about hypocrisy. Some doubted the existence of God; others doubted the effectiveness of the church. As I struck up correspondence with several of my readers, I found that most of the time it wasn't the weight of the questions themselves that burdened their faith but rather the notion that they shouldn't be asking them, that it wasn't allowed. What was happening on my blog was happening on many others. It was happening in living rooms and churches, in coffee shops and bars, in the US and around the world. The environment was changing, and Christianity was changing with it.

I didn't really know what it was like to be on the outside of the evangelical bubble looking in until the fall of 2008, when I voted for Barack Obama.

I wasn't exactly a fanatic. I had no Shepard Fairey "Hope" posters on my bedroom wall, no Obama/Biden bumper stickers on my car. I disagreed with some of Obama's positions, particularly concerning abortion, and I had concerns about his experience. But on most issues, including health care, foreign policy, the environment, poverty, and the economy, I preferred his perspective to John McCain's. I also admired his leadership style and ability to communicate.

I'm no shrinking violet when it comes to talking politics, but even I was overwhelmed by the hostile responses I received from many of my conservative friends. I was called a socialist and a baby killer. People questioned my commitment to my faith and my country, some suggesting that I may face eternal consequences for my decision at the ballot box. One friend compared Barack Obama to Osama Bin Laden, another suggested he might be the Antichrist, and another asked why I would vote for someone who would undoubtedly usher in the great tribulation. Women I respected called Hillary Clinton crude names and made jokes about her going to hell. A Christian coworker said he thought Ted Kennedy's brain tumor was a result of divine intervention. I got email after email with subject lines like "Jesus Hates Welfare" and "Vote Your Christian Values." Pastors and teachers implied that my decision at the ballot box was the most important decision I would make all year.

As far as I'm concerned, the teachings of Jesus are far too radical to be embodied in a political platform or represented by a single candidate. It's not up to some politician to represent my Christian values to the world; it's up to me. That's why I'm

always a little perplexed when someone finds out that I'm not a
Republican and asks, "How can you call yourself a Christian?"

It seems that a whole lot of people, both Christians and
non-Christians, are under the impression that you can't be a
Christian and vote for a Democrat, you can't be a Christian and
believe in evolution, you can't be a Christian and be gay, you
can't be a Christian and have questions about the Bible, you can't
be a Christian and be tolerant of other religions, you can't be a
Christian and be a feminist, you can't be a Christian and drink
or smoke, you can't be a Christian and read the *New York Times*,
you can't be a Christian and support gay rights, you can't be a
Christian and get depressed, you can't be a Christian and doubt.
In fact, I am convinced that what drives most people away from
Christianity is not the cost of discipleship but rather the cost
of false fundamentals. False fundamentals make it impossible
for faith to adapt to change. The longer the list of requirements
and contingencies and prerequisites, the more vulnerable faith
becomes to shifting environments and the more likely it is to
fade slowly into extinction. When the gospel gets all entangled
with extras, dangerous ultimatums threaten to take it down
with them. The yoke gets too heavy and we stumble beneath it.

Centuries before anyone had ever heard of biological evolution, Saint Augustine warned of creating false fundamentals in
regard to our interpretation of the book of Genesis. "In matters
that are so obscure and far beyond our vision," he wrote, "we
find in Holy Scripture passages which can be interpreted in very
different ways without prejudice to the faith we have received.
In such cases, we should not rush in headlong and so firmly take

our stand on one side that, if further progress in the search for truth justly undermines this position, we too fall with it."[14]

Through the blog, I encountered all kinds of people, young and old, who no longer considered themselves Christians because of false fundamentals. "I took a biology class and was convinced that the theory of evolution was sound," said one. "I'm tired of fighting the culture wars," said another. "I couldn't live with the thought of all non-Christians going to hell," said another. I'm frustrated and sad to think of all the good people who have abandoned Christianity because they felt they had to choose between their faith and their intellectual integrity or between their religion and their compassion. I'm heartbroken to think of all the new ideas they could have contributed had someone not told them that new ideas were unwelcome.

Of course, we all carry around false fundamentals. We all have unexamined assumptions and lists of rules, both spoken and unspoken, that weigh down our faith. We've all got little measuring sticks that help us determine who's "in" and who's "out," and we've all got truths we don't want to face because we're afraid that our faith can't withstand any change. It's not just conservative Christians. Many of us who consider ourselves more progressive can be tolerant of everyone except the intolerant, judgmental toward those we deem judgmental, and unfairly critical of tradition or authority or doctrine or the establishment or whatever it is we're in the process of deconstructing at the moment. In a way, we're all fundamentalists. We all have pet theological systems, political positions, and standards of morality that are not essential to the gospel but that we cling to so tightly that we leave fingernail marks on the palms of our hands.

Jesus said, "Come to me, all you who are weary and burdened, and I will give you rest. Take my yoke upon you and learn from me, for I am gentle and humble in heart, and you will find rest for your souls. For my yoke is easy and my burden is light" (Matt. 11:28 – 30).

Once, a guy asked Jesus about his yoke, or teaching. He asked Jesus what he thought was the most important of all the Jewish laws. Jesus, who often responded to one question with another, chose this time to answer the man directly.

He said, " 'Love the Lord your God with all your heart and with all your soul and with all your mind.' This is the first and greatest commandment. And the second is like it: 'Love your neighbor as yourself.' All the Law and the Prophets hang on these two commandments" (Matt. 22:37 – 40).

Love.

It's that simple and that profound. It's that easy and that hard.

Taking on the yoke of Jesus is not about signing a doctrinal statement or making an intellectual commitment to a set of propositions. It isn't about being right or getting our facts straight. It is about loving God and loving other people. The yoke is hard because the teachings of Jesus are radical: enemy love, unconditional forgiveness, extreme generosity. The yoke is easy because it is accessible to all — the studied and the ignorant, the rich and the poor, the religious and the nonreligious. Whether we like it or not, love is available to all people everywhere to be interpreted differently, applied differently, screwed up differently, and manifested differently. Love is bigger than faith, and it's bigger than works, for it inhabits and transcends both.

The apostle John, who is described in the Gospels as "the disciple whom Jesus loved," explained it like this in his letter to Christian churches across Asia Minor: "Dear friends," he wrote, "let us love one another, for love comes from God. Everyone who loves has been born of God and knows God. Whoever does not love does not know God, because God is love.... No one has ever seen God; but if we love one another, God lives in us and his love is made complete in us" (1 John 4:7 – 8, 12).

How ironic that the most important fundamental element of the Christian faith is something that is relative, something that cannot be measured with science, systematized with theology, or managed with rules. How fitting and how strange that God should hide his biggest secret in that present yet elusive thing that poets and artists and musicians and theologians and philosophers have spent centuries trying to capture in some form but that we all know the minute we experience it. How lovely and how terrible that absolute truth exists in something that cannot really be named.

One of my favorite TV series of all time is BBC's *Planet Earth*. I love it because narrator David Attenborough can make a colony of cockroaches feeding on a hundred-meter-high mound of bat dung sound like the most wonderful thing in the world, and I love it because it shows how magnificently living organisms can adapt to their environments. From the extra-thick eyelashes of the wild Bactrian camel, to the dense white fur of the Arctic hare, to the sticky yellow toes of the gliding leaf frog, each animal has its unique way of thriving in its habitat, be it a dusty desert, a snowy tundra, or the tops of trees.

Take cave angelfish, for example. These little fish are perhaps the most specialized creatures on earth, as they've specifically adapted for life in cave waterfalls. While marine angelfish are known throughout the world for their colorful fins and attractiveness in aquariums, cave angelfish are ugly as sin. Having lost the pigment in their skin, they look more like ghostly, winged snakes than fish. Microscopic hooks on their fins allow them to cling to cave walls like bats. Positioned just right, they can feed on bacteria rushing down the waterfalls. Their eye sockets are empty, their bodies elongated and slimy.

Scientists believe that a group of marine angelfish must have migrated to the caves millions of years ago to escape predators or to adjust to climate change. Like many cave dwellers, over the years they evolved blindness and improved other sensory functions because in their environment eyesight was no longer useful. Cave angelfish live exclusively in a few remote caves in Thailand, and the *Planet Earth* crew went to all kinds of trouble to capture footage of these little survivors in their natural habitat. Of course, Attenborough — who I imagine looks a bit like Bilbo Baggins — makes it sound as though they'd discovered Middle Earth.

Cave angelfish illustrate how survival isn't always pretty. Sometimes it involves growing claws on fins, or going blind in order to see. My story isn't pretty either. It isn't even finished yet. But I'm telling it because it's the best evidence I've got in support of my theory of evolution, that faith must adapt in order to survive.

The apostle Paul wrote to the Corinthians that "if anyone is in Christ, he is a new creature; the old things passed away; behold, new things have come" (2 Cor. 5:17 NASB). Followers of Jesus Christ are a transitional species. The Christian life, on both an individual and a collective level, is comprised of an awkward assemblage of the old and the new, the necessary and the unnecessary, the good and the bad, the sinful and the redeemed. Adapting to a new environment is challenging because it's hard to know which fundamentals are false and need to be shed and which fundamentals are truly essential and need to develop and grow. I'm sure that at times we look a little strange, like angelfish clinging to the walls of a cave.

I'm not yet thirty, but I feel as if over the past few years, my faith has experienced a lifetime of change. I've rethought some of my fundamental beliefs about the Bible, salvation, science, religion, the cosmic lottery, Jesus, and truth. The process has been ugly at times, but each day I feel a little closer to having the kind of faith that can survive the volatility of constant change, the kind of faith that can outlive my doubt and fear. I can't always say that I feel closer to God — the doubts often return — but I think I'm finally beginning to understand that it's me who's moving, not him. Like salvation, evolution is an everyday process. I'm still changing, and I expect I always will be.

CHAPTER 20

Dan the Fixer

My husband, Dan, is the kind of guy people listen to. This is because he is quiet most of the time, right most of the time, and six foot four all of the time. He chooses his words carefully and usually waits until he has something meaningful to contribute to the conversation before jumping in. I love that he always raises the level of discourse, not with heavy-handed opinions but with good questions. Even when he knows the answer, he prefers to wait until asked to share his thoughts.

It's a well-known fact that Dan can fix just about anything — cars, computers, toilets, TVs, websites, wireless adapters, busted RC planes, beat-up trucks, broken jewelry, you name it. Smart, resourceful, and attentive to detail, Dan's a born troubleshooter. So when he decided to take a stab at the real estate market by flipping a foreclosed 1930s fixer-upper in downtown Dayton, I knew he could do it.

We loved that little Craftsman bungalow, regardless of the fact that the paint was peeling, the columns sagging, and it looked like it was getting eaten by a nearby tree. An uprooted sidewalk led to a crumbling porch, which led to a squeaky door, which led to a complete disaster inside. Original hard-wood floors lay beneath a layer of dust and an old carpet that smelled of cat urine and mildew. Dozens of windows needed to be replaced. The bathrooms were unusable, as water had rotted through the floors and left murky brown puddles in the bath-tubs and the toilets. Someone had started painting the walls a seaweed green but stopped right in the middle of a stroke.

Despite its first impression, the house felt solid and had a great floor plan, and we got it at a good price. Dan jumped right in, ripping into the floors, reframing walls, and replacing the porch. He spent hours in a dark crawl space under the house, with just an inch or two between his nose and the floor joists. Once, he punched a hole in a wall, and cockroach feces poured out like sand from an hourglass. He bumped into weird remind-ers of the home's previous owners: a naked Barbie in the laundry room, old pictures in a bedroom, a prescription suppository box behind the toilet. He came home smelling of plaster, dirt, and sweat.

There were times when I worried he wasn't moving fast enough. I didn't see my meticulously chosen paint colors on the walls or my bargain-store mirrors over the sinks. On the outside, things looked like they actually were getting worse, not better. Tools, debris, and pieces of two-by-fours lay scattered on the floor, and you could taste the gypsum dust in the air. But Dan had it all planned out: demo, repairs, finishing. I had to "respect the process" and hold off on the aesthetics until later. Essentials first. The whole thing reminded me of something my mother used to say during spring cleaning, when we reorganized our closets and pulled all the stuff out from under our beds. "Sometimes it has to get messy before it can be cleaned."

We thought the whole process would take about six months, which in house-flipping time means it took about a year. However, we managed to sell it for a profit during the worst real-estate market of our lifetimes. By the time Dan was done, it was the prettiest house on the street, with clean, slate-colored siding, light blue accents, new windows, a freshly reconstructed porch, and shiny black house numbers on one of the columns. I took before and after pictures as if we were on HGTV.

One of the greatest gifts Dan has ever given me was to respond to my struggle with doubt with the same "respect for the process" that he brought to the flip. It was natural for people to want to fix me on the outside, to quiet or scold me or to warn me to stop asking so many questions. But Dan seemed to understand better than anyone that this was a necessary path on my journey of faith. Through my petulance and insecurity, my tears and my rage, through my longest nights and darkest days, he listened, asked questions, offered his shoulder, and patiently saw me through. I guess he just knew that sometimes it has to get messy before it can be cleaned.

CHAPTER 21

Living the Questions

Once, when I was small, my eczema flared up so badly that I couldn't sleep. I tossed and turned in my bed for hours, frantically scratching my arms and legs until they bled onto the sheets. Every hour or so, I called for my mother or father, who rotated the task of lathering my body with lotion and putting fresh, cool socks over my hands. Sometimes they prayed with me. Sometimes they held me or stroked my hair as I cried into my pillow.

At some point in the night, just as my father was about to leave me after another rotation, I asked him why God let this happen to me, why God didn't make my eczema go away. I remember that he stood by my bedroom door, where the soft glow of my nightlight illuminated his face and the lines on his forehead. I remember that he had tears in his eyes.

"I don't know," he said, after clearing his throat. "But I know that he loves you."

He turned away, gently closed the door, and I listened to his slow, heavy footsteps trigger creaks in the floorboards all the way to the living room. My father, who had committed his life to Christian education, who could read the Old Testament in Hebrew and the New Testament in Greek, who had a shelf full of commentaries and a wall full of diplomas, who delivered beautiful sermons and wrote eloquent papers, didn't know.

At first I was angry; then I was fearful. But as I lay in the dark, scratching and crying and praying, I realized that no other answer would have been right. No other answer could do justice to the question. Twenty years later, I'm convinced it is the most important thing my father ever told me.

I used to think that the measure of true faith is certainty. Doubt, ambiguity, nuance, uncertainty — these represented a lack of conviction, a dangerous weakness in the armor of the Christian soldier who should "always be ready with an answer."

With the best of intentions, the generation before mine worked diligently to prepare their children to make an intelligent case for Christianity. We were constantly reminded of the superiority of our own worldview and the shortcomings of all others. We learned that as Christians, we alone had access to absolute truth and could win any argument. The appropriate Bible verses were picked out for us, the opposing positions summarized for us, and the best responses articulated for us, so that we wouldn't have to struggle through two thousand years of theological deliberations and debates but could get right to the bottom line on the important stuff: the deity of Christ, the nature of the Trinity, the role and interpretation of Scripture, and the fundamentals of Christianity.

As a result, many of us entered the world with both an unparalleled level of conviction and a crippling lack of curiosity.

So ready with the answers, we didn't know what the questions were anymore. So prepared to defend the faith, we missed the thrill of discovering it for ourselves. So convinced we had God right, it never occurred to us that we might be wrong.

In short, we never learned to doubt.

Doubt is a difficult animal to master because it requires that we learn the difference between doubting God and doubting what we believe about God. The former has the potential to destroy faith; the latter has the power to enrich and refine it. The former is a vice; the latter a virtue.

Where would we be if the apostle Peter had not doubted the necessity of food laws, or if Martin Luther had not doubted the notion that salvation can be purchased? What if Galileo had simply accepted church-instituted cosmology paradigms, or William Wilberforce the condition of slavery? We do an injustice to the intricacies and shadings of Christian history when we gloss over the struggles, when we read Paul's epistles or Saint Augustine's *Confessions* without acknowledging the difficult questions that these believers asked and the agony with which they often asked them.

If I've learned anything over the past five years, it's that doubt is the mechanism by which faith evolves. It helps us cast off false fundamentals so that we can recover what has been lost or embrace what is new. It is a refining fire, a hot flame that keeps our faith alive and moving and bubbling about, where certainty would only freeze it on the spot.

I would argue that healthy doubt (questioning one's beliefs) is perhaps the best defense against unhealthy doubt (questioning

God). When we know how to make a distinction between our
ideas about God and God himself, our faith remains safe when
one of those ideas is seriously challenged. When we recognize
that our theology is not the moon but rather a finger pointing at
the moon, we enjoy the freedom of questioning it from time to
time. We can say, as Tennyson said,

> Our little systems have their day;
> They have their day and cease to be;
> They are but broken lights of thee,
> And thou, O Lord, art more than they.[15]

I sometimes wonder if I might have spent fewer nights in
angry, resentful prayer if only I'd known that my little systems
— my theology, my presuppositions, my beliefs, even my fundamentals — were but broken lights of a holy, transcendent God. I
wish I had known to question them, not him.

What my generation is learning the hard way is that faith is
not about defending conquered ground but about discovering
new territory. Faith isn't about being right, or settling down, or
refusing to change. Faith is a journey, and every generation con-
tributes its own sketches to the map. I've got miles and miles to
go on this journey, but I think I can see Jesus up ahead.

Occasionally people will ask me what I think about truth. They
ask me if I believe in it, what I think it is, and if I think it's relative or absolute. These are pretty sophisticated questions to ask

someone who once lost her contact lens in her eye ... for two days.

I have a feeling that what people are really asking is, Do you think that Christians are right and everybody else is wrong? I guess I'm just not ready to give an answer about that because I'm still not sure if that's the point.

I suppose that if absolute truth exists, it must be something that we experience indirectly, like the sun. We see it in shadows, watch it light up the moon, and feel it tingle our skin, but it's generally not a good idea to try to stare at it or claim it as one's own. Every now and then, when I'm reading the Bible or Emily Dickinson, I think I've bumped into it. But when I try to tell Dan about it, it doesn't come out right. I think I see little pieces of it in all the people I know — in Nathan, in Laxmi, in Adele, even in June. I believe it is embodied in the person of Jesus Christ, which means it is relational, because everyone experiences Jesus a little differently.

I'm no longer ready to give an answer about everything. Sometimes I'm not ready because I feel that an answer does not do justice to the seriousness or complexity of the question. Sometimes I'm not ready to give an answer because I honestly don't know what the best one is. Sometimes I'm not ready to give an answer because I can tell that the person asking doesn't really want one anyway.

Unfortunately, saying "I don't know" has fallen out of vogue in Christian circles, and I'm still trying to get used to saying it myself. Opinionated and strong-willed, I'm always afraid that if I remain silent or show signs of ambivalence, people will assume that I can't think for myself, that I haven't studied an issue or thought it through. As my friends well know, I'll tolerate a barrage of vicious insults before I'll tolerate the mere suggestion that I might be uninformed. I would rather people think I don't bathe enough than think I don't read enough.

In a way, the same has been true of the church of late. Sometimes Christians worry that if we don't provide bullet-point answers to all of life's questions, people will assume that our faith is unreasonable. In reaction to very loud atheists like Richard Dawkins, we have become a bit too loud ourselves. Faith in Jesus has been recast as a position in a debate, not a way of life.

But the truth is, I've found people to be much more receptive to the gospel when they know becoming a Christian doesn't require becoming a know-it-all. Most of the people I've encountered are looking not for a religion to answer all their questions but for a community of faith in which they can feel safe asking them.

When Peter first penned the words "always be ready with an answer," he was writing to the persecuted church during the time of the emperor Nero. It was a very dangerous time to be a Christian, as Nero liked to blame everything that went wrong in the Roman Empire, including the great fire in 64 AD, on followers of Christ. According to tradition, Peter himself was brutally crucified. Writes Peter, "Who is going to harm you if you are eager to do good? But even if you should suffer for what is right, you are blessed. 'Do not fear what they fear; do not be frightened.' But in your hearts set apart Christ as Lord. Always be prepared to give an answer to everyone who asks you to give the reason for the hope that you have. But do this with gentleness and respect, keeping a clear conscience, so that those who speak maliciously against your good behavior in Christ may be ashamed of their slander. It is better, if it is God's will, to suffer for doing good than for doing evil" (1 Peter 3:13 – 17).

This was not advice for a debate team; it was advice for martyrs! Peter asked his readers to take courage, to look into the eyes of their assailants with patience and compassion, gentleness and respect. He urged them to live lives that are beyond reproach, to follow the teachings of Jesus Christ and love their enemies to the point of death. This passage is not about fearlessly defending a set of propositions; it's about fearlessly defending hope — a wild, bewitching, and reckless thing that cannot be systematized or proven or rationally explained.

Peter knew that such behavior might arouse some curiosity. He knew that his fellow Christians would be subject to interrogation regarding their radical community and unconventional lives. In preparing them to give answers, Peter assumed they'd be asked questions. Our best answers in defense of Christianity have always been useless clanging symbols unless our lives have inspired the world to ask.

My friend David, who has a doctorate in philosophy but is cool and understated about it, put it this way: "Belief is always a risk, a gamble — an adventure, if you will. The line between faith and doubt is the point of action. You don't need certainty to obey, just the willingness to risk being wrong."

He wrote that on my Facebook wall.

One of my favorite poets, Rainer Rilke, shared this advice with a young writer: "Have patience with everything that remains unsolved in your heart. Try to love the questions themselves, like locked rooms and like books written in a foreign language. Do not now look for the answers. They cannot now be given to you because you could not live them. It is a question of experiencing everything. At present you need to live the question. Perhaps you will gradually, without even noticing it, find yourself experiencing the answer, some distant day."[16]

There are a lot of things I don't know. I don't know where evil came from or why God allows so much suffering in the world. I don't know if there is such a thing as a "just war." I don't know how God will ultimately judge between good and evil. I don't know which church tradition best represents truth. I don't know the degree to which God is present in religious systems, or who goes to heaven and who goes to hell. I don't know if hell is an eternal state or a temporary one or what it will be like. I don't know which Bible stories ought to be treated as historically accurate, scientifically provable accounts of facts and which stories are meant to be metaphorical. I don't know if it really matters so long as those stories transform my life. I don't know how to reconcile God's sovereignty with man's free will. I don't know what to do with those Bible verses that seem to condone genocide and the oppression of women. I don't know why I have so many questions, while other Christians don't seem to have any. I don't know which of these questions I will find answers to and which I will not.

And yet slowly I'm learning to love the questions, like locked rooms and mysterious books, like trees that clap their hands and fish that climb up cave walls, like mist that clings to the foothills of the Himalayas just like it clings to the Appalachians. And slowly I am learning to live the questions, to follow the teachings of a radical rabbi, to live in an upside-down kingdom in which kings are humbled and servants exalted, to look for God in the eyes of the orphan and the widow, the homeless and the imprisoned, the poor and the sick. My hope is that if I am patient, the questions themselves will dissolve into meaning, the answers won't matter so much anymore, and perhaps it will all make sense to me on some distant, ordinary day.

Those who say that having childlike faith means not asking questions haven't met too many children. Anyone who has kids or loves kids or has spent more than five minutes with kids knows that kids ask a lot of questions. Rarely are they satisfied with short answers, and rarely do they spend much time absorbing your response before moving on to the next "why?" or "how come?"

Psychologists say that the best way to handle children in this stage of development is not to answer their questions directly but instead to tell them stories. As pediatrician Alan Greene explains, "After conversing with thousands of children, I've decided that what they really mean is, 'That's interesting to me. Let's talk about that together. Tell me more, please.'"[17]

Questions are a child's way of expressing love and trust. They are a child's way of starting dialogue. They are a child's way of saying, "I want to have a conversation with you."

So when a little girl asks her father where the moon came from, he might tell her that the moon circles around the earth and reflects light from the sun. He might tell her that the moon likes to play hide-and-seek with the sun, so sometimes the moon looks like it's peeking out from behind a black curtain; sometimes all you can see is the top of its head, and sometimes you can't even see it at all! He might tell her about how the moon has invisible arms that can pull the oceans back and forth, making tides rise and fall. He might tell her that astronauts have walked on the moon and played golf on the moon and collected rocks from the moon. He might tell her that the moon has dimples and craters and basins that we can see only with a telescope and that there's a special place on the moon called the Sea of Tranquility that isn't really a sea. Then the father might take the little girl outside, hoist her up onto his shoulders, and let her stare at the moon for a while. He might recite a poem about a cow jumping over the moon or sing a song about a dreamy-eyed kid slow-dancing with it. Soon the little girl will become so lost in her father's beautiful stories that she will forget she ever had a question to begin with.

If there's one thing I know for sure, it's that serious doubt — the kind that leads to despair — begins not when we start asking God questions but when, out of fear, we stop. In our darkest hours of confusion and in our most glorious moments of clarity, we remain but curious and dependent little children, tugging frantically at God's outstretched hands and pleading with every question and every prayer and every tantrum we can muster, "We want to have a conversation with you!"

God must really love us, because he always answers with such long stories.

Acknowledgments

Thank you, Rachelle Gardner, for taking a chance on a new author and a strange title. Thanks to the good folks at Zondervan — especially Angela, Brian, Mike, Laura, and Beth — for bringing your expertise and creativity to the project while preserving so much of its integrity. Thank you, Ben Williams, for looking over my proposal, and Christian George, for mentioning it to WordServe. Much love to the community of readers at *RachelHeldEvans.com* that inspired so much of this book and will no doubt inspire another.

Special thanks to those friends whose stories I have shared alongside mine. The beauty and complexity of your lives far surpass the titles that I gave you — soldier, apologist, feminist, widow, oxymoron, best friend. You have influenced me in more ways than can be squeezed into a chapter and have blessed me in more ways than can be squeezed into words.

I am more grateful than ever to the teachers who pushed me the hardest and encouraged me the most: Colleen Boyett, Connie Landreth, Richard Daugherty, Kari Ballentine, Ray Legg, Whit Jones, Beth Impson, John Carpenter, and Ruth Kantzer.

Special thanks to the Bryan College family and to the good people of Dayton for making Monkey Town such a lovely place to call home.

Mom, Dad, and Amanda — thank you for teaching me to be curious, to ask questions, and to take leaps of faith. Thank you for making the chapters about my childhood so easy to write and enjoyable to read.

Dan — your name should be on the cover next to mine because this book wouldn't exist without you. Thank you for urging me to pursue my passions, for cheering me on when I got discouraged, for not losing faith even when I did, for sacrificing, for listening, for encouraging, and for loving unconditionally. I couldn't have asked for a better life partner, and I can't wait to see what new adventures await us.

Notes

1. William J. Bouwsma, *John Calvin: A Sixteenth-Century Portrait* (Oxford: Oxford University Press, 1988), 72.

2. Edward J. Larson, *Summer for the Gods: The Scopes Trial and America's Continuing Debate over Science and Religion* (Cambridge: Harvard University Press, 1997), 88–89.

3. Ibid., 14.

4. Kurt P. Wise, *Faith, Form, and Time: What the Bible Teaches and Science Confirms about Creation and the Age of the Universe* (Nashville: Broadman and Holman, 2002).

5. Kurt P. Wise, "Geology," *In Six Days: Why Fifty Scientists Choose to Believe in Creation* (Green Forest, Ariz.: John F. Ashton, 2000), 353.

6. Josh McDowell, *Evidence That Demands a Verdict* (San Bernardino, Calif.: Here's Life, 2004), 10.

7. David Noebel, *Understanding the Times* (Manitou Springs, Colo.: Summit, 1991), 841.

8. Conversations with Andy represent a composite of several conversations with more than one individual.

9. Jonathan Edwards, "Sinners in the Hands of an Angry God," *Wikisource, the Free Library*, http://en.wikisource.org/wiki/Sinners_in_the_Hands_of_an_Angry_God (accessed September 2, 2009).

10. Anne Lamott, *Traveling Mercies* (New York: Anchor, 2000), 3.

11. C. S. Lewis, *Mere Christianity* (New York: HarperCollins, 2001), 64.

12. N. T. Wright, *Surprised by Hope* (New York: HarperOne, 2008), 18 – 19.

13. Rob Bell, *Velvet Elvis: Repainting the Christian Faith* (Grand Rapids: Zondervan, 2005), 43.

14. Saint Augustine, *The Literal Meaning of Genesis*, translated and annotated by John Hammond Taylor, S.J. (New York: Newman, 1982), 1:41.

15. Alfred Tennyson, "In Memoriam A. H. H.," *Wikisource, the Free Library*, http://en.wikisource.org/wiki/In_Memoriam_A._H._H. (accessed September 2, 2009).

16. Rainer Maria Rilke, *Letters to a Young Poet* (Toronto: Random House of Canada, 1986), 34.

17. Alan Greene, "Why Children Ask 'Why,'" *DrGreene.com*, March 13, 2000: http://www.drgreene.org/body.cfm?id=21&action=detail&ref=564 (accessed September 2, 2009).